The Gospel of Saint Luke

Dedication: I want to dedicate this book to my wife, Paula who has encourage me as I wrote this missive. I also want to dedicate it to all the teachers, professors, and friends that have helped me understand the message of Luke's gospel.

Most importantly I want to thank The Holy Spirit who has opened my mind to many new ideas, and helped me see that ministering to others and living a Christ like life is how we should spend our days during this life.

Cover painting: detail from "Saint Luke Drawing the Virgin"
by Rogier de la Pasture van der Weyden,
Flemish Northern Renaissance painter born in 1399 or 1400.

Table of Contents

The Gospel of Saint Luke
A Devotional Commentary

Introduction

In this book you will find the text of the Gospel of Luke, from the New Testament. It is my intention to insert my thoughts concerning different passages between verses of the Holy Text. These will consist of my feelings, and comments about what is found there.

As you will notice I have selected the King James Version of the scripture as the basis for this study. I choose this edition of the scriptures because it is the one I am most familiar with, it is the one I have a computer copy of (which will facilitate this process), and most importantly, while archaic in its usage of the English language, it is also the most lyric and pleasing to those who like me, love the way its authors string words together. As the old adage goes: Done right, a sentence can set the soul soaring, done wrong and it can set the soul snoring. The men who translated the King James Version did the former.

* * *

One of the goals of the Reformation was to do away with the Latin version of the scriptures, called the Vulgate, and substitute it with a version that was in the language of the common people. In Germany, Luther performed the task. In England it was done by scholars who were working for King James. In other countries other men did it. Translating the scripture into the language of the common people was a noble goal. However, one must remember that The King James Version was translated at a time when most people, possibly 95%, were illiterate. While the authors desired to create a Bible in the language of the people, the vast majority of the average men and women were unable to read it for themselves and would instead be hearing it read to them by their pastors and other educated church leaders. For that reason the translators wrote it in a manner that lent itself to being read aloud, worded it in a lyric manner that would trip off the tongue lightly and easily. So while they could have been more literal in their translation from the Greek and Latin, they chose not to, instead favoring a choice of words that would sound good, a choice of words that the writer in me also likes best, because the language soars.

* * *

This commentary is not meant to be any kind of scholarly work. I will consult other authors rarely, if at all. What you will get is just the scriptural text and my understanding of it. I may sometimes check a reference or a book to see if my memory serves me well. I may even from time to time do a little research before pontificating on a verse or passage. However, and for the most part, it is not my intention to do any preparation for this commentary. What you will find are just my thoughts on the scriptures. Someone I shared a portion of this with said I was teaching. No, not so. I am only offering opinion. I get very

4

emotional about some topics, but my opinions and my emotions do not necessarily equate with truth. What you will get in this devotional commentary is just my thoughts.

I choose this approach because I think Heavenly Father is offended by deep spiritual studies that go on and on seeking meaning in every little thing contained in the scriptures. Like the King James Version, the Bible and the Book of Luke in particular, are meant for the people, not the scholars. We should not need someone with a degree in Theology to lead us through God's word. Just our own common sense and the promptings of the Holy Spirit should be enough. In fact, I think that we will find that our common sense will often be at odds with what theologians and scholars tell us to believe. So, you will find no teachings in this work, just thoughts and ideas. I make no claims to the veracity of what you will read, I just claim its sincerity.

Be warned, I am a frail ordinary man with more faults than I care to own up to. I do not offer these thoughts on Luke's gospel out of any illusion that I am special myself, or that I have any extraordinary insights as to the gospel's meaning. My thoughts are my own. I have studied the scriptures a great deal and read many books. The occasional use of these previously written sources does not exclude inspiration and revelation on my part. Rather, it enhances my understanding that God works through inspired individuals to bring forth His scriptures as they carefully choose which material to include. For instance, a recurring theme I expect you will see is that the Christianity Luke presents does not consist of a bunch of doctrines but is the story of a life and a style of living.

Joseph Smith said of The Book of Mormon: "A man would get nearer to God by abiding by its precepts, than by any other book." I hope this work will help readers get nearer to God too. I do not want it to fill your head with ideas. This is not an intellectual work. Instead I

*want it to fill your heart with a desire to live a Christlike life, a life of
ministry to your fellow men, women, and children. In fact, this book is
my attempt to minister to you, my reader.*

*During the closing days of her life, Mother Teresa was having some
difficulty getting around. A man, hearing of her problem, carved her a
walking stick. She sent him a thank you letter which I will quote: Thank
you very much for the walking stick, so beautifully carved. My
gratitude is my prayer for you, that you may allow by God's grace to
carve Word of God on your soul, on your mind, so that you may become
more and more like Him, Jesus the Word made Flesh who loved us unto
the very limit of love, the cross*

It is that becoming more and more like Him that this book is about.

Below you will find the scripture in normal black print, such as this. *I
will not be able to comment on everything. Much I do not understand,
other has been adequately explained by others, and finally some does
not lend itself to the devotional tone I seek for this work. So my plan is
to put the text of Luke's gospel down and then high light in* **Bold** *any
thing I want write about. Then in italics, such as you see here, I will put
down my thoughts on what moved me as I read that particular section
of the text. I intend that on one hand, this be personal and I do not want
to hold back, yet I also want this to be read by others. It is not just for
me. For the above reason, I must be on display here, warts and all,
otherwise this becomes a waste of time, or even worse, an ego trip. So
then plan on finding my faults, foibles, and unorthodoxies all on
display. My personal struggle as a man, and priest will also be here in
hopes that someone else may profit from my understandings as well as
my triumphs and failings.*

    Let us begin.

Chapter 1

1 FORASMUCH as many have taken in hand to set forth in order a declaration of those things which are most surely believed among us,
2 Even as they delivered them unto us, which from the beginning were eyewitnesses, and ministers of the word;
3 It seemed good to me also, having had perfect understanding of all things from the very first, to write unto thee in order, most excellent Theophilus,
4 That thou mightest know the certainty of those things, wherein thou hast been instructed.

What a gift! A perfect understanding of Christ's life. I am not sure I even understand my own life. One of my reasons for this writing is to gain a better comprehension of myself and my savior. Hopefully my meditations on Luke will end in both readers and myself least having a better knowledge of our Savior and His life. Even though we will not attain Luke's level of perfect comprehension, it is my prayer that this book will result in both reader and author having a deeper and more spiritual understanding of Christ and that we will be challenged by that learning to be more Christlike in our thoughts and actions.

* * *

I wanted to avoid controversy, at least at the beginning of this tome. However, the text is not going to let me. We need to answer the question of the origin of this book. Luke claims that he wrote it. Others will say no, that it was written by the Holy Spirit or Heavenly Father. It is a question that needs exploring, but I just don't think the very beginning of this commentary is the proper time and place. So I will handle that issue in the Appendix at the end of this book. I encourage you to leave it till later and instead immerse yourself in this gospel's wonderful first chapter.

5 ¶ THERE was in the days of Herod, the king of Judæa, a certain priest named Zacharias, of **the course of Abia**: and his wife *was* of the daughters of Aaron, and her name *was* Elisabeth.

At this time in history the Tribe of Levi had grown so large that there were too many priests for the jobs to be done in the temple. To solve the problem they were divided up into groups or as they are called here "courses." The priests in these courses stayed in whatever village they called home until such time as it was their course's turn to work in the temple. They then went to Jerusalem, served in God's House, and then returned home till their turn came up again.

Sadly, this problem does not exist today, and in fact we have men and women called to serve full time in our temples, because there is more work to do than there are priests and their wives who show up to do it. A regrettable state of affairs. I myself am a case in point, and I realize I need to attend more often.

6 **And they were both righteous before God, walking in all the commandments and ordinances of the Lord blameless.**

This must have been some couple. Both righteous and blameless! What an inspiration they must have been to those who knew them. While I do not believe that we will achieve perfection in his life, it seems that this couple demonstrated that the opportunity is there for us to get close. Zacharias and Elizabeth seem to have done pretty well. If they can be righteous before God and walk in His commandments and ordinances, then so can we.

A man and his wife working together as a team to serve God and His people can accomplish great things. A case in point is my conversion and baptism. When I was investigating the Church I was taught by a senior couple who's name was Harris. His name was Grant, sadly I do not recall her first name. They were very special people and I thank God I met them, that they took an interest in me, and the Holy Spirit inspired me to listen to them. I had chased off more young missionaries than I could count but when this special couple came along I was powerless before them. They are the closest I have come to meeting a pair like Zacharias and Elizabeth. I suspect many of you will also have met such couples, devoted to serving their fellow men and God in heaven.

It is interesting to note, as a side bar, that Grant Harris was a direct descendant of Martin Harris of Book of Mormon fame. He confirmed me. I was baptized by a different man than Grant, because he was too elderly to put me under and lift me out of the baptismal waters. This other man was a direct descendant of Parley Pratt, another "great" of the early church.

7 **And they had no child, because that Elisabeth was barren, and they both were *now* well stricken in years.**

This must have been quite hard for them to understand and to accept. We just read where they were righteous. In Biblical times barrenness was seen as a curse or punishment for sins. Zacharias and Elizabeth were the best people they could be, and better than most around them yet she cannot get pregnant. This had to be a real trial of their faith.

I am put in mind of the Hymn "Farther Along." The hymn goes:

Tempted and tried, we're oft made to wonder
Why it should be thus all the day long;
While there are others living about us,
Never molested, though in the wrong.

- o *Refrain:*
  Farther along we'll know more about it,
  Farther along we'll understand why;
  Cheer up, my brother, live in the sunshine,
  We'll understand it all by and by.

Sometimes I wonder why I must suffer,
Go in the rain, the cold, and the snow,
When there are many living in comfort,
Giving no heed to all I can do.

  Farther along we'll know more about it,
  Farther along we'll understand why;
  Cheer up, my brother, live in the sunshine,
  We'll understand it all by and by.

Tempted and tried, how often we question
Why we must suffer year after year,
Being accused by those of our loved ones,
E'en though we've walked in God's holy fear.

  Farther along we'll know more about it,
  Farther along we'll understand why;
  Cheer up, my brother, live in the sunshine,
  We'll understand it all by and by.

*Might not thoughts like this or something similar have filled their
hearts. I think they must have.*

8 And it came to pass, that **while he executed the priest's office**
   before God in the order of his course,
9 According to the custom of the priest's office, **his lot was to
   burn incense when he went into the temple of the Lord**.

*I believe that this means he was alone in the temple. It had different
chambers, an outer one called the Holy Place and an inner one
separated from outer one by a heavy veil. This inner one was called the
Holy of Holies and only the High Priest went in there and only once a
year. Zacharias was not the High Priest and not in the Holy of Holies.
Nevertheless there is a wonderful confluence here, a nexus, if you will.
Zacharias is in a sacred spot, and doing his sacred dut when he is
visited. Heavenly Father could have sent the angel to him any time or
place. That He chose this time and place I do not think is a coincidence.
If we want a heavenly visitation, we should be doing what we are
supposed to be doing, it is then that we will most likely get it. That
Zacharias was in the temple, I believe was also a facilitating factor.
There is no other place closer to the Lord, nor a better place to hear
Him.*

10 And **the whole multitude of the people were praying without
    at the time of incense**.
11 And there appeared unto him an angel of the Lord standing on
    the right side of the altar of incense.

Again, here the nexus grows, Here is another reason I think the timing of the angelic visit is no coincidence. The people are outside praying. This activity on their part would be pleasing to Heavenly Father and also worked to make the time propitious for the angelic visit. (It is interesting to note that Zacharias was burning incense at this time too, incense being a type or symbol of prayer. The sweet smelling smoke rising toward heaven is a picture of a believer's prayers). So, we find here a confluence of factors that are working together. Prayer by the people, Zacharias burning incense (a type of prayer) and he also being about the Lord's business, and that business taking place in the temple. All these ingredients combine to make this a perfect time for an angelic visit.

Do you or I want inspiration? It can come anytime and any place. But isn't it more likely to come when we are in the Lord's house, about His work, and in an attitude of prayer?

A personal story might be in order here. I knew a man named BrotherTalley back in the early 1980's. He was a Stake High Councilman. His wife got cancer. He was a righteous man and prayed and prayed for her. It was his practice, as often as possible, to visit her in the hospital after he finished his job. One day he felt inspired to go to the temple instead of the hospital and do work for the dead. That day he worked in the Baptistery and was baptized and confirmed for about fifty people. As he was leaving the temple somehow one of those dead people for whom he had done the work that day spoke to him and told him that fifty new church members were now praying for his wife. That is so special. All these years later, that still brings tears to my eyes as I read my own writing about it. Those are the experiences which make your religion not just something you talk about, but it becomes real. It changes your life, it makes you into a new person. That is when your religion gets right down next to where the real you live. You do God's work and are blessed for it.

12 And when Zacharias saw *him,* **he was troubled, and fear fell upon him**.

In Biblical times it was thought if you saw an angel it meant you were about to die. This would explain his fear.

13 But the angel said unto him, Fear not, Zacharias: for thy prayer is heard; and thy wife Elisabeth shall bear thee a son, and thou shalt call his name John.

14 And thou shalt have joy and gladness; and many shall rejoice at his birth.

15 For he shall be great in the sight of the Lord, and shall drink neither wine nor strong drink; and **he shall be filled with the Holy Ghost, even from his mother's womb**.

This seems to contradict most explanations I have heard on how to get the filling of the Holy Spirit. I think most people believe there is a difference between the "gift of the Holy Ghost" and the "filling of the Holy Ghost." The gift being a positional thing that comes with baptism and church membership which entitles you to guidance from the Holy Spirit as you seek to live a righteous life. Joseph Smith and Oliver Cowdery testify that after their baptisms they had a much clearer understanding of the scriptures and what they were translating. Before their baptism they had Josephs abilities as a seer to help them, but after baptism they had the Holy Spirit as a guide too.

The filling of the Holy Ghost is something different, a sometimes ecstatic feeling comes at deeply spiritual moments in ones life. In my church we are taught that the "Gift" of the Holy Spirit, comes with the laying on of hands following baptism. The "Filling" is something else and I am not sure how it is acquired. Other churches have people receive either the filling or the gift or both in other ways. However, regardless, of which church's beliefs we are talking of, the filling of the Holy Spirit is a gift reserved for righteous people who are committed church members. An new born baby does not seem to fit the mold for any church's doctrine on who gets and how they get filled. Do we mark John down as a special case or do we throw out all our ideas on how and when a person can be filled with the Holy Spirit? I am opting for the special case.

16 And many of the children of Israel shall he turn to the Lord their God.
17 And he shall go before him in the spirit and power of Elias, to **turn the hearts of the fathers to the children, and the disobedient to the wisdom of the just; to make ready a people prepared for the Lord.**

The angel seems to be making a prophesy about what John would do. It was a job that he wouldn't complete during his life in New Testament times. He came back about two hundred years ago, appeared to Joseph Smith, and gave him the priesthood and the power for us to do temple work for our dead.

18 **And Zacharias said unto the angel, Whereby shall I know this? For I am an old man, and my wife well stricken in years.**

It seems an innocent enough question, given Elizabeth's barrenness and both of their age. Yet, as we will see, it gets a rise out of the angel. The lesson here would seem to be that when Heavenly Father tells us something we should not second-guess Him. Instead, we should just be accepting. Kind of runs contrary to our human natures, but there it is. Zacharias acts human and as we shall see he is going to pay a price for his lack of faith.

19 And the angel answering said unto him, **I am Gabriel, that stand in the presence of God; and am sent to speak unto thee, and to shew thee these glad tidings.**
20 **And, behold, thou shalt be dumb, and not able to speak, until the**

day that these things shall be performed, because thou believest not my words, which shall be fulfilled in their season.

Gabriel seems to lack humility and to get a little huffy. He seems to say to Zacharias, "Hey, do you know who I am, I am Gabriel. I stand in God's presence. He sent me here to tell you these glad tidings." Then there is an implied, "And since you chose to doubt," followed by the penalty to be paid.

I find it interesting that angels always appear as male figures. If my suspicions are correct, maybe as we come to respect women more and more, Heavenly Father will start to send them on angelic missions.

21 And the people waited for Zacharias, and marvelled that he tarried so long in the temple.
22 And when he came out, he could not speak unto them: and they perceived that he had seen a vision in the temple: for he beckoned unto them, and remained speechless.
23 And it came to pass, that, as soon as the days of his ministration were accomplished, he departed to his own house.
24 And after those days **his wife Elisabeth conceived, and hid herself five months, saying,**
25 **Thus hath the Lord dealt with me in the days wherein he looked on** *me,* **to take away my reproach among men.**

I detect a bit of doubt on Elisabeth's part here too. She must have been afraid she would not be able to carry the child to term. I guess that she would face even more reproach if she got pregnant and then lost the child, than if she had never gotten pregnant at all. Yet at the same time you find her hiding, you also see her rejoicing in her pregnancy. All her life she has no doubt longed for this to happen. Now it has and it is almost too good to be true. God has blessed her, but she fears to count her chickens before they hatch. I see in these verses a woman who is very happy, but having had a lifetime of guilt about not being a mother, she is afraid to let herself fully enjoy the blessing of her pregnancy.

Most of us, at least those of us who have had sorrows, are a lot like Elisabeth. We enjoy the good when it happens, but we are wary of letting ourselves get too comfortable. We know how transitory the good can be. We can only hope that the good is with us more than the bad. We enjoy the good while we can but don't let ourselves settle into a state of contentment. It is a truism that: "Religion starts where joy and pain intersect."

26 And **in the sixth month** the angel Gabriel was sent from God unto a city of Galilee, named Nazareth,

There are other clues in the scriptures, but this is the first intimation that Jesus was not born in December, but rather the spring. If we assume Mary becomes pregnant soon after Gabriel's visit in the sixth month and the gestation period for Him was the normal one, then He should be born in the third month of the following year.

27 To a **virgin** espoused to a man whose name was Joseph, of the house of David; and the **virgin's** name *was* Mary.

The fact that Mary was a virgin brings up an interesting point. Allow me to digress here for a few paragraphs. It is important to remember that prophecy can be for two groups of people. The New Testament takes Isaiah's prophecy (Isaiah 7:14) and applies it to Mary and Jesus. However a careful reading of that original prophecy in context clearly says that the people to whom a prophecy was given can expect a sign will be given to them, and that sign is that a virgin will conceive and have a child, call him Immanuel and before he is old enough to know good from evil a certain other prophecy will come to pass.

What happened was, the Israelites of Isaiah's day were told something (given a prophesy), and then told ask for a sign to prove that it was true. The king refused to ask for a sign and so he is told that he will get one anyway and this is it, a virgin shall conceive… etc. It is something he is told to look for so he will know Isaiah's words were true. It would hardly work, or make sense, if it only came to pass over 600 years after he died. It is therefore safe to say that there was a virgin birth long before Christ's.

So then prophecy, at least in this case, and in many others, if not all, has two audiences. Those to whom it is given, and those who come later. It is also interesting to note that if my analysis is correct, most catholic and protestant theologians are wrong in their assumption that Christ's birth was unique in respect to Mary, and the fact that she was both a virgin and pregnant at the same time. There was at least one virgin birth prior to Mary having Jesus..

True, scholars of the Hebrew language tell us the word Isaiah uses could be translated virgin or just young woman, but in light of how the verse is quoted in the New Testament I think we clearly have to opt for former. I guess we just verged on the heretical again. Alas the words take us where they take us. I can't forget an old axiom taught me somewhere along the line: When the plain sense of scripture makes common sense, seek no other sense.

28 And the angel came in unto her, and said, **Hail, *thou that art* highly favored, the Lord *is* with thee: blessed *art* thou among women**.

I would imagine Mary is about 15 at this time. Knowing teenagers as I do, this is indeed high praise. She must have been a very special girl. I had a girl like that in my Sunday School class once. She was a little younger (13) than I would guess Mary was here, yet such a sweet, dedicated, and spiritual child. One example of this: I remember her having the prettiest long hair. She always kept her hair neat and clean and you could tell a lot of time went into taking care of it. She must have known, that as Paul states, it was her glory (I Cortnyhian11:15). One Sunday she showed up with it cut short. I was terribly disappointed in her for cutting it until I found out she had (at her own volition -- she had not been pressed to do so) donated her lovely hair to have in made into a wig for a cancer patient, and not even a cancer patient she knew, but just some poor stranger who was suffering the loss of her hair.

29 And when she saw *him,* she was troubled at his saying, and cast in her mind what manner of salutation this should be.
30 And the angel said unto her, Fear not, Mary: for thou hast found favour with God.
31 And, behold, thou shalt conceive in thy womb, and bring forth a son, and shalt call his name **JESUS**.

Jesus means saviour. Jews of this time were apt to give their children names with religious significance.

32 He shall be great, and shall be called the Son of the Highest: and the Lord God shall give unto him the throne of his father David:
33 And he shall reign over the house of Jacob forever; and of his kingdom there shall be no end.
34 Then said Mary unto the angel, **How shall this be, seeing I know not a man**?

It seems a little strange that Zacharias was punished for asking just such a question and yet Mary isn't even corrected. There seems to be a double standard in operation here. Why?

35 And the angel answered and said unto her, The Holy Ghost shall come upon thee, and the power of the Highest shall overshadow thee: therefore also that holy thing which shall be born of thee shall be called the Son of God.

36 **And, behold, thy cousin Elisabeth, she hath also conceived a son in her old age: and this is the sixth month with her, who was called barren.**

We mentioned earlier that Elizabeth went into hiding when she started to show. It would seem she did not even tell her family she was pregnant, for the angel would not tell Mary things the angel knew she was already well aware of.

37 For with God nothing shall be impossible.
38 And Mary said, Behold the handmaid of the Lord; be it unto me according to thy word. And the angel departed from her.
39 And Mary arose in those days, and went into the hill country with haste, into a city of Juda;
40 And entered into the house of Zacharias, and saluted Elisabeth.
41 **And it came to pass, that, when Elisabeth heard the salutation of Mary, the babe leaped in her womb; and Elisabeth was filled with the Holy Ghost:**
42 **And she spake out with a loud voice, and said, Blessed *art* thou among women, and blessed *is* the fruit of thy womb.**
43 **And whence *is* this to me, that the mother of my Lord should come to me?**
44 **For, lo, as soon as the voice of thy salutation sounded in mine ears, the babe leaped in my womb for joy.**
45 **And blessed *is* she that believed: for there shall be a performance of those things which were told her from the Lord.**

This whole scene is a little confusing. For it to work, we have to make some assumptions. It does not seem that Elisabeth would have had any way of knowing what had happened to Mary. Therefore it seems that when she was filled with the Holy Spirit, the Spirit must told her of the angel's visit to Mary and that her young cousin carried the Messiah in her womb.

46 And Mary said, **My soul doth magnify the Lord,**

47 **And my spirit hath rejoiced in God my Saviour.**

48 **For he hath regarded the low estate of his handmaiden: for, behold, from henceforth all generations shall call me blessed.**

49 **For he that is mighty hath done to me great things; and holy** *is* **his name.**

50 **And his mercy** *is* **on them that fear him from generation to generation.**

51 **He hath shewed strength with his arm; he hath scattered the proud in the imagination of their hearts.**

52 **He hath put down the mighty from** *their* **seats, and exalted them of low degree.**

53 **He hath filled the hungry with good things; and the rich he hath sent empty away.**

54 **He hath holpen his servant Israel, in remembrance of** *his* **mercy;**

55 **As he spake to our fathers, to Abraham, and to his seed for ever.**

The forgoing is a poem. That Mary would write one about what had happened to her is not unusual. Many people, women especially, are of a poetic nature. It does seem passing strange, however, that the poem should be the first words out of her mouth when Elisabeth greets her. I would guess that there is a time gap between verses 45 and 46 even though at first reading it would not seem to be so.

*The poem's inclusion here brings up another interesting wrinkle concerning the matter of to what level are the scriptures inspired. Mary says **henceforth all generations shall call me blessed.** Most people believe those words to be true, to be prophetic (After all they do seem to have come to pass!). Yet we have to ask what level of inspiration is going on here. Is it limited to Luke giving us an accurate rendition of Mary's poem, or are the words of her poem inspired too? I have noticed a pattern among the dogmatists among us. When they find a person* *quoted in the scriptures and when they like what he or she says, those words can and do become the basis of doctrine. Yet are they really meant to be that, or are we just reading an inspired rendering of their words? Are we mistakenly basing our beliefs on what is only an accurate accounting of a speech that may, in fact, be full of mistakes? Food for thought.*

Henceforth all generations shall call me blessed. *Another thought here, to have been the inspiration for a piece of music like Schubert's **Ave Maria** is indeed to be blessed. In that musical piece alone her prophesy has been fulfilled. I am not Roman Catholic, but I request that that piece of music be part of any memorial service held for me.*

56 And Mary abode with her about three months, and returned to her own house.

57 Now Elisabeth's full time came that she should be delivered; and she brought forth a son.

58 And her neighbours and her cousins heard how the Lord had shewed great mercy upon her; and they rejoiced with her.

59 And it came to pass, that on the eighth day they came to circumcise the child; and they called him Zacharias, after the name of his father.

60 And his mother answered and said, Not *so;* but he shall be called John.

61 And they said unto her, There is none of thy kindred that is called by this name.

62 And they made signs to his father, how he would have him called.

63 And he asked for a writing table, and wrote, saying, His name is John. And they marvelled all.

64 And his mouth was opened immediately, and his tongue *loosed,* and he spake, and praised God.

This must have been quite a scene, one of my favorites in all the scriptures. I do not think I can add to it, but I want to say how inspiring I find it. I would love to have been there.

65 And fear came on all that dwelt round about them: and all these sayings were noised abroad throughout all the hill country of Judæa.
66 And all they that heard *them* laid *them* up in their hearts, saying, What manner of child shall this be! And the hand of the Lord was with him.
67 And his father **Zacharias was filled with the Holy Ghost, and prophesied, saying,**
68 **Blessed** *be* **the Lord God of Israel; for he hath visited and redeemed his people,**
69 **And hath raised up an horn of salvation for us in the house of his servant David;**
70 **As he spake by the mouth of his holy prophets, which have been since the world began:**
71 **That we should be saved from our enemies, and from the hand of all that hate us;**
72 **To perform the mercy** *promised* **to our fathers, and to remember his holy covenant;**
73 **The oath which he sware to our father Abraham,**
74 **That he would grant unto us, that we being delivered out of the hand of our enemies might serve him without fear,**
75 **In holiness and righteousness before him, all the days of our life.**
76 **And thou, child, shalt be called the prophet of the Highest: for thou shalt go before the face of the Lord to prepare his ways;**
77 **To give knowledge of salvation unto his people by the remission of their sins,**
78 **Through the tender mercy of our God; whereby the dayspring from on high hath visited us,**
79 **To give light to them that sit in darkness and** *in* **the shadow of death, to guide our feet into the way of peace.**

What we have here is a rite very much like that practiced in the Church of Jesus Christ of Latter Day Saints today. The boy is given a name and a blessing. Zacharias, like fathers today, takes the child up in arms and declares just how the child will be known, what their name will be. Following that the father then gives his child a blessing using the power of the priesthood to make declarations about the child's future.

Like Mary's words above to Elisabeth, this is a poetic passage, one of the very few in the New Testament. Unlike Mary's, however, we learn his words are prophesy, given if not by, then with the guidance of the Holy Spirit. Again I have to wonder how "inspiration" worked here and how much "inspiration" was involved. Was Zacharias poetic to start with, and Heavenly Father chose to use this bent on the part of his priest, or was Heavenly Father in a poetic mood himself when the Holy Spirit was sent to Zacharias so He gave him the words of his prophesy in Zacharias' version of iambic pentameter?

Another thing I would draw your attention to are Zacharias's words: **he spake by the mouth of his holy prophets, which have been since the world began.** *Heavenly Father had Prophets since Adam's time up until Christ's time. Why should He change that. Yet, without any scripture to back up such a claim, many churches say there are no more prophets. I believe that is wrong. Why limit God in His tools to give us inspiration and guidance?*

80 And the child grew, and waxed strong in spirit, and was in the deserts till the day of his shewing unto Israel.

*An interesting chapter, Luke's first, it was full of spiritual food **and** food for thought. The characters we met were wonderful people. All in all, however, I have to say this chapter makes one wonder just how* *inspiration works. The way I have been taught does not seem to comport with the actuality we find here. I also want to mention that I had always just taken it for granted that angels were some sort of perfect beings. However, Gabriel does not fit into the mold of perfection very well. He comes off as both haughty and inconsistent. Well, he was not without his faults when he walked the world as Noah either. Finally, we also find quite a few instances of filling by the Holy Spirit, and none fit with common church teachings on how that is accomplished. Lesson learned: Things are not always as we have been taught, and that we should turn to Heavenly Father and not some theologian for wisdom.*

Chapter 2

1 AND it came to pass in those days, that there went out a decree from Cæsar Augustus, that all the world should be taxed.
2 (*And* this taxing was first made when Cyrenius was governor of Syria.)
3 **And all went to be taxed**, every one into his own city.

What is that old saying about death and taxes.

4 And Joseph also went up from Galilee, out of the city of Nazareth, into Judæa, unto the city of David, which is called Bethlehem; (**because he was of the house and lineage of David**:)

Both Joseph and Mary were descendants of David. I have heard some claim that Jesus would have been entitled to David's throne, had David's family still ruled Israel. I do not believe this to be true. When you read the genealogies found in this and other gospels, it seems that Joseph was not the oldest son of the oldest son etc. all the way back to David. Also, it was not always the king's oldest son that always took the throne on the death of the king anyway. Solomon is a case in point. So, to claim that Jesus was entitled to the throne is a stretch. Besides, the promise to David and Abraham before him was only that the Messiah would come from their loins, not necessarily by primogeniture.

It should also be mentioned that Jewishness is determined by the mother. You are Jewish if your mother was. This is the custom, because in almost all cases there is a bit of doubt as to whom the father of any child is. That's the reason I believe Mary's genealogy is also included in the gospels. The Pharisees would later taunt Christ about who his father was, but they never (so far as we know) called his either Jewishness or him being of the House of David into question. They couldn't, because everyone knew Mary was his mother, and Mary was descended from David.

5 To be taxed with Mary his espoused wife, being great with child.
6 And so it was, that, while they were there, the days were accomplished that she should be delivered.
7 And she brought forth her firstborn son, and wrapped him in swaddling clothes, **and laid him in a manger; because there was no room for them in the inn.**

I have always felt that it is neat that Heavenly Father chooses to use the humble and lowly to confound the mighty. He sends his son to be born in a stable. He speaks in a still, small voice, out of a burning bush, touching our heart and giving us a warm sensation of revelation.

Today, it is the thundering preachers, delivering sermons with lots of histrionics that get the attention. When Jesus taught he sat down to deliver his message. It is content, not delivery style that is important. That is one reason I so enjoy our church. I have been a member for almost forty years and have yet to hear a hellfire and brimstone message, nor a speaker working himself or herself up into a lather. Instead I hear thoughtful, soul searching, wisdom from the pulpit.

8 And there were in the same country shepherds **abiding in the field, keeping watch over their flock by night.**

I understand that this only happens for a few weeks during the season when the lambs are being born. Then the shepherds stay with their flocks around the clock in case one of the ewes needs assistance. The rest of the year the shepherds were in bed at night in their home or maybe a tent if the pasturage was out in the wilderness. Lambs are born in the spring, and if the foregoing is true, then it is safe to assume that Christ was born in the spring, and not December.

9 And, lo, the angel of the Lord came upon them, and the glory of the Lord shone round about them: and they were sore afraid.
10 And the angel said unto them, Fear not: for, behold, I bring you good tidings of great joy, which shall be to all people.
11 For unto you is born this day in the city of David a Saviour, which is Christ the Lord.
12 And this *shall be* a sign unto you; Ye shall find the babe wrapped in swaddling clothes, lying in a manger.
13 And suddenly there was with the angel a multitude of the heavenly host praising God, and saying,
14 Glory to God in the highest, and on earth peace, good will toward men.
15 And it came to pass, as the angels were gone away from them into heaven, the shepherds said one to another, Let us now go even unto Bethlehem, and see this thing which is come to pass, which the Lord hath made known unto us.
16 And they came with haste, and found Mary, and Joseph, and the babe lying in a manger.
17 And when they had seen *it,* they made known abroad the saying which was told them concerning this child.
18 And all they that heard *it* wondered at those things which were told them by the shepherds.
19 **But Mary kept all these things, and pondered *them* in her heart.**

You just have to wonder what was going on in this young woman's heart. Too be singled out like she has been. To be a virgin and then get pregnant and finally deliver.

*How full Mary's heart must have been with all that had happened to
her in the last nine months. Luke says she pondered them. I guess so!
What life changing experiences. She was, as we were told above,
singled out because she was highly favored, yet even a special young
woman like her must have marveled at all that was happening to her.
She may not be worthy of the level of veneration the Roman Catholic
Church heaps upon her, but she clearly must stand head and shoulders
above other young women of her day and ours. Indeed, a very special
young woman.*

20 And the shepherds returned, glorifying and praising God for all the
things that they had heard and seen, as it was told unto them.
21 And when eight days were accomplished for the circumcising of the
child, his name was called JESUS, which was so named of the angel
before he was conceived in the womb.
22 **And when the days of her purification according to the law of
Moses were accomplished, they brought him to Jerusalem, to
present *him* to the Lord;**

*I believe that this period is about 30 days. It was a strange custom of
the Jewish (and I believe other cultures of that time period and maybe
on until today). At any rate, women were considered unclean during the
time each month of their menstruation, due to their bleeding.
Childbirth, however, being a much more bloody affair took longer to
get over (or get clean again). Women were not able to mix with society
for a long period after giving birth.*

23 (As it is written in the law of the Lord, Every male that openeth the
womb shall be called **holy to the Lord**;)

*Once Mary could again be considered clean (see above) she and
Joseph wasted no time in taking Christ to the temple. This hurry on
their part is not to be wondered at. A child like him should be taken*

there as soon as possible. The temple is "Holy unto the LORD" and so is this child.

24 And to offer a sacrifice according to that which is said in the law of the Lord, A pair of turtledoves, or two young pigeons.
25 And, behold, there was a man in Jerusalem, whose name *was* Simeon; and the same man *was* just and devout, **waiting for the consolation of Israel: and the Holy Ghost was upon him.**
26 **And it was revealed unto him by the Holy Ghost, that he should not see death, before he had seen the Lord's Christ.**
27 **And he came by the Spirit into the temple: and when the parents brought in the child Jesus, to do for him after the custom of the law,**
28 **Then took he him up in his arms, and blessed God, and said,**
29 **Lord, now lettest thou thy servant depart in peace, according to thy word:**
30 **For mine eyes have seen thy salvation,**

Scripture study can be a knowledge gathering time or it can be a life changing experience. Simeon can be an old man who God told that he would get to see the Messiah before he died, but he can be so much more if we use our empathy to try and feel what Simeon felt. I try and put myself in his shoes. I try to imagine how he felt. When I do it moves me deep in my soul. Simeon becomes more than just an old man I envisage. He becomes me and I him and together we go to the temple and we look and look for couple with a baby that they are bringing to present to the Lord. Not just any baby. The baby God gave us a personal promise about. The baby that would grow to be the Messiah and save His people. The Messiah that would save our family, that would save the world. When you put yourself in the story like that it becomes so much more real. Instead of dry facts, it can become a life changing experience for you personally.

*Simeon "**waits**" means more than we think of as waiting. I believe that there is an implied constant prayer on the man's part that the Messiah will come. He asks God about it so often, that he is finally told that it will happen in his lifetime. Then one day the Spirit comes over him and tells him his prayer is answered, that the Messiah has been born, and if he goes to the temple he can see the child. Think of what this must have meant to Simeon. A bittersweet. It could mean his death was imminent, but at the same time the thing he has longed for and sought was about to happen. He was going to see the Messiah. Many times true Christians are asked to put their own welfare second to that of their fellow beings. Just so, Simeon, the coming of the Messiah is so much more important than any other consideration. The thing he lived for is about to happen and he must have been very excited as he went to the temple. There he waits, watching the crowds. Was he one who mistakenly expected the Christ to be rich and noble in birth? Did he get excited when he saw a wealthy couple coming in with a child? Did he already know that Heavenly Father likes to use the simple things to confound the mighty. Whatever his expectations were, we know that when he saw Joseph and Mary with the baby Jesus, that the Holy Spirit told him that here was the answer to his prayers. We know that when he saw Mary and Joseph and Jesus that he took the young child up in his arms. As he did so he poured out his soul in a prayer and thanksgiving. One has to wonder how he felt, holding what had been the focus of his spiritual life in his hands. I expect there was a feeling of ecstasy. I love it myself when the spirit moves me for some reason. It gives me a little taste of what Simeon was feeling.*

Mary had seen many strange things in her life over the last year. Here was another one. A strange man comes up to her and wants to hold her baby. She lets him, for she must know that here is a devout man who understands just who Mary's son is.

31 Which thou hast prepared before the face of all people;

32 A light to lighten the Gentiles, and the glory of thy people Israel.

33 And Joseph and his mother marvelled at those things which were spoken of him.

34 And Simeon blessed them, and said unto Mary his mother, Behold, this *child* is set for the fall and rising again of many in Israel; and for a sign which shall be spoken against;

35 (Yea, a sword shall pierce through thy own soul also,) that the thoughts of many hearts may be revealed.

36 And there was one Anna, a prophetess, the daughter of Phanuel, of the tribe of Aser: she was of a great age, and had lived with an husband seven years from her virginity;

37 And she *was* a widow of about fourscore and four years, which departed not from the temple, but served *God* with fastings and prayers night and day.

This woman was quite old, one hundred and six or thereabouts. Even more interesting is the fact she is identified as a prophet. I can think of only one other woman in the Bible that is called a "prophetess" and that is Deborah in the book of Judges. From this we can make two deductions, one that female prophets are rare, and two that they do exist.

First the rarity: It has been my observation that women have more of a natural spiritual instinct than men have. They seem to gravitate to the spiritual much more easily than their male counterparts. So why then, are not more of them prophets (which I take to be a spiritual level higher than most of us will achieve)? I do not know, unless there is a spiritual glass ceiling imposed by society. A ceiling that Heavenly Father may not approve of, but at least works with. Without some such explanation it is hard to understand how a group with more innate spiritual abilities find themselves limited in how high they can rise in spiritual rank, while those with less natural spiritual leanings leap frog over the stronger to take the leadership positions. Could it be that

Heavenly Father knows our short comings as a society, and rather than try to make wholesale changes in how we do things and our prejudices, chooses to work within them, letting the gospel enlighten us gradually. History shows that things have gotten better under Christianity, even if it has been a slow process filled with more mistakes and misdirections than we would like to remember. For instance, because of Muslim influence women throughout Near East and Europe were allowed much less freedom and fewer privileges than they had known when Europe was ruled by Rome. Then about the year 1000 Catholic veneration of Mary the Mother of Jesus began. Prior to that time, while looked up to, she was not seen with the same esteem as she now enjoys. However, when Catholics came to worship her it had an effect on all women, seeing them rise and rise over time till today where women and men are seen as almost equals.

38 And she coming in that instant gave thanks likewise unto the Lord, and spake of him to all them that looked for redemption in Jerusalem.
39 And when they had performed all things according to the law of the Lord, they returned into Galilee, to their own city Nazareth.
40 And the child grew, and waxed strong in spirit, filled with wisdom: and the grace of God was upon him.
41 **Now his parents went to Jerusalem every year at the feast of the passover.**

Joseph and Mary were devout. Taking a 120 mile walk (round trip) is not something many people are apt to do unless they have to.

42 And when he was twelve years old, they went up to Jerusalem after the custom of the feast.
43 **And when they had fulfilled the days, as they returned, the child Jesus tarried behind in Jerusalem; and Joseph and his mother knew not *of it.***

44 But they, supposing him to have been in the company, went a day's journey; and they sought him among *their* kinsfolk and acquaintance.

This section seems to me to speak to an unusual relationship between Christ and his earthly parents. I cannot feature them taking off for home and just assuming that He was with them. This is not how caring parents treat their children. If, however, your child is also the Son of God, that might put a different spin on things. It seems obvious that Mary and Joseph treated Christ differently.

45 And when they found him not, they turned back again to Jerusalem, seeking him.
46 And it came to pass, that after three days they found him in the temple, sitting in the midst of the doctors, both hearing them, and asking them questions.
47 And all that heard him were astonished at his understanding and answers.
48 And when they saw him, they were amazed: and his mother said unto him, **Son, why hast thou thus dealt with us? behold, thy father and I have sought thee sorrowing.**
49 And he said unto them, How is it that ye sought me? Wist ye not that I must be about my Father's business?

Here again, we see the unusual relationship. Mary asks why he stayed behind without a word to them. It would only have been common courtesy between adults, and without a doubt expected of a son or daughter. Christ's answer seems to dismiss their concerns without giving them any weight at all. I fail to understand it. Mary shows up again and again through out Chirst's life and at his death, He provided for her by giving one of his disciples responsibility for her. He must have cared for the woman and she for Him, but only secondarily. His ministry came first. Maybe this is an example of what we later find Him

50 And they understood not the saying which he spake unto them.
51 And he went down with them, and came to Nazareth, and was subject unto them: but his mother kept all these sayings in her heart.
52 And Jesus increased in wisdom and stature, and in favour with God and man.

Chapter 3

1 **Now in the fifteenth year of the reign of Tiberius Cæsar, Pontius Pilate being governor of Judæa, and Herod being tetrarch of Galilee, and his brother Philip tetrarch of Ituræa and of the region of Trachonitis, and Lysanias the tetrarch of Abilene,**
2 **Annas and Caiaphas being the high priests**, the word of God came unto John the son of Zacharias in the wilderness.

This is a data dump by Luke. Why do I need to know that at the time he is about to tell me of, that Lysanias was tetrarch of Abilene? Why do I need to know who all these other officials were too? I have pondered this question and I think maybe Luke is trying to establish his scholarship. Remember how he opened his gospel? He told us that many people had decided to write books about Christ's life, and he felt compelled to do so too. As an author, I can tell you that if you write a book on a subject you want your book to the one people read. So too, Luke wants his book to stand out. This might be one way to make his book the authoritative one. Anyone who can tell you who was who as far as politicians holding different offices were, must have a real grasp of facts, or at least that is the impression Luke may be trying to give. (This again brings us back to "Inspiration" and how it works. The above can and possibly does explain Luke's inclusion of arcane data. If Heavenly Father were just using Luke as a word processor, however, why the inclusion? Heavenly Father does not have anything to prove, and we should pay attention to His words regardless. So I once more see evidence that "Inspiration" does not come in the manner we have been taught.)

3 And he came into all the country about Jordan, preaching the baptism of repentance for the remission of sins;

4 As it is written in the book of the words of Esaias the prophet, saying, The voice of one crying in the wilderness, Prepare ye the way of the Lord, make his paths straight.

5 Every valley shall be filled, and every mountain and hill shall be brought low; and the crooked shall be made straight, and the rough ways *shall be* made smooth;

6 And all flesh shall see the salvation of God.

7 **Then said he to the multitude that came forth to be baptized of him, O generation of vipers, who hath warned you to flee from the wrath to come?**

8 **Bring forth therefore fruits worthy of repentance,** and begin not to say within yourselves, We have Abraham to *our* father: for I say unto you, That God is able of these stones to raise up children unto Abraham.

John looks around himself and finds it has apparently become popular to be baptized. It is the thing to do. It is the ancient equivalent of the modern evangelical church's altar call. But John is not satisfied to just dunk them and then publish his "saved" numbers. He knows that many, if not most, of those he is baptizing go into the Jordan River a dry sinner and come out a wet one. There is more to getting religion than recognizing a need. There is change involved, repentance, and new direction in life.

Conversion is a life changing experience. The Catholics say "For godly sorrow worketh repentance to salvation not to be repented of." The Church of Jesus Christ of Latter Day Saints teaches that one must "endure to the end." I think both are saying the same thing. Salvation is not just coming down an aisle at church, praying for forgiveness, and then returning to pretty much the same life. It is life changing. Salvation is being born again. Becoming a new person in Christ. Not only that, but it lasts too. I remember taking Greek in college and in Greek there is a "present pluperfect tense" that has "abiding effects into the future." You do whatever it is now in the present, but the action effects the future too. So to, just getting "saved" in the present tense is not enough, you have to be "saved" in the present pluperfect tense. A "saved" that has abiding effects into your future.

I want to be careful not to give the wrong impression here. I am not talking about perfection. That is not what Heavenly Father expects of us. No body achieves that. But I am speaking of an attempt to do right. An Elder of my church, J. Golden Kimbal, said it well. "I may not stay on the Straight and Narrow all the time, but I cross it a lot."

9 And now also the axe is laid unto the root of the trees: every tree therefore which bringeth not forth good fruit is hewn down, and cast into the fire.

10 And the people asked him, saying, What shall we do then?

11 He answereth and saith unto them, **He that hath two coats, let him impart to him that hath none; and he that hath meat, let him do likewise.**

It is a theme of the Gospel that riches have little place among believers. This is a tenant that the church has gotten away from. The Puritans who help found this country believed it was Godly to be rich. Much of the modern church feels the same. There are whole faiths built around the idea that if you give to God (usually there is a pastor who is nice enough to become God's surrogate and accept the money for Him), God will return the favor by giving you riches. It is a religious Ponzi scheme. Think about it, that is exactly what it is. You put in a little bit of money and get back a lot. A religion where greed is the guiding principal.

Years ago, before I became a Latter Day Saint I attended a church just outside Washington D,C. The pastor had the church purchase a very nice home for his parsonage and he drove a brand new Cadillac, Why? He said that people were more likely come and follow him and join his church if he seemed prosperous. This is not the gospel that Christ taught. Getting rich isn't the goal. Just how does the getting of wealth and the giving away of your earthly possessions blend together. Does Christ want us to be Bill Gates and Warren Buffets, and become billionaires first and then having great wealth turn to philanthropy? I do not think that is what John and later Christ was talking of. I think they both taught that service to your fellow man or woman is what we should be about now. Philanthropy is not for the future either, it should be an everyday practice of the devout.

12 Then came also publicans to be baptized, and said unto him, Master, what shall we do?

13 And he said unto them, Exact no more than that which is appointed you.

14 And the soldiers likewise demanded of him, saying, And what shall we do? And he said unto them, Do violence to no man, neither accuse *any* falsely; and be content with your wages.

15 And as the people were in expectation, and all men mused in their hearts of John, whether he were the Christ, or not;

16 John answered, saying unto *them* all, I indeed baptize you with water; but one mightier than I cometh, the latchet of whose shoes I am not worthy to unloose: he shall baptize you with the Holy Ghost and with fire:

17 Whose fan *is* in his hand, and he will throughly purge his floor, and will gather the wheat into his garner; but the chaff he will burn with fire unquenchable.

18 And many other things in his exhortation preached he unto the people.

19 But Herod the tetrarch, being reproved by him for Herodias his brother Philip's wife, and for all the evils which Herod had done,

20 Added yet this above all, that he shut up John in prison.

It seems things are out of order here. John can't baptize Jesus if he is rotting in jail.

21 Now when all the people were baptized, it came to pass, that **Jesus also being baptized, and praying, the heaven was opened,**
22 **And the Holy Ghost descended in a bodily shape like a dove upon him, and a voice came from heaven, which said, Thou art my beloved Son; in thee I am well pleased.**
23 **And Jesus himself began to be about thirty years of age, being (as was supposed) the son of Joseph, which was *the son* of Heli,**

I have to wonder why Joseph's geneology is included starting in the verse above and continuing below. Since the clear teaching of the scripture is that he was not Jesus' physical father, of what importance is his line? Nevertheless, Jews and LDS people love their genealogies. So, you got it, why not include it. After all, the Old Testament has chapter after chapter of geneology. Also, its inclusion may be another attempt by Luke to show that his gospel is authoritative. At any rate, this chapter concludes by giving us Joseph's genealogy all the way back to Adam.

Also of interest, this is one of the few times in scripture we find all three members of the Godhead together in the same place at the same time. Jesus is being baptized. The Holy Ghost appears as a dove. Heavenly Father speaks. Many churches put great stock in the idea of a "Trinity" and the assertion that all three parts of the "Trinity" are really one and that they are co-equal and co-eternal. They go so far as to claim that acceptance of this "doctrine" is necessary for salvation. I think not. Any doctrine that important would be laid out in detail somewhere in the scriptures. However, it does not appear. It is inferred. Now I will allow those that believe in the trinity to believe in it if they like. I do not think it is of any great import one way or the other.

24 Which was *the son* of Matthat, which was *the son* of Levi, which was *the son* of Melchi, which was *the son* of Janna, which was *the son* of Joseph,

25 Which was *the son* of Mattathias, which was *the son* of Amos, which was *the son* of Naum, which was *the son* of Esli, which was *the son* of Nagge,

26 Which was *the son* of Maath, which was *the son* of Mattathias, which was *the son* of Semei, which was *the son* of Joseph, which was *the son* of Juda,

27 Which was *the son* of Joanna, which was *the son* of Rhesa, which was *the son* of Zorobabel, which was *the son* of Salathiel, which was *the son* of Neri,

28 Which was *the son* of Melchi, which was *the son* of Addi, which was *the son* of Cosam, which was *the son* of Elmodam, which was *the son* of Er,

29 Which was *the son* of Jose, which was *the son* of Eliezer, which was *the son* of Jorim, which was *the son* of Matthat, which was *the son* of Levi,

30 Which was *the son* of Simeon, which was *the son* of Juda, which was *the son* of Joseph, which was *the son* of Jonan, which was *the son* of Eliakim,

31 Which was *the son* of Melea, which was *the son* of Menan, which was *the son* of Mattatha, which was *the son* of Nathan, which was *the son* of David,

32 Which was *the son* of Jesse, which was *the son* of Obed, **which was *the son* of Boaz, which was *the son* of Salmon,** which was *the son* of

Naasson,

33 Which was *the son* of Aminadab, which was *the son* of Aram, which was *the son* of Esrom, **which was *the son* of Phares, which was *the son* of Juda,**

Both Mary and Joseph where descendants of the Old Testament's King David. So they and Christ through Mary have much the same genealogy, it only dividing some generations after David. I find it interesting that while we do not know much about the people listed in the genealogy, most are just a name, nevertheless there are a few exceptions. We know even less about the wives and mothers of these men listed as Christ's forefathers. In fact, we know of only three women in the line of Christ between Jacob and David, a period of hundreds of years. However, when the Bible does speak of them they turn out to be very interesting women.

For instance, Phares was the son of Judah by Tamar. Tamar was not a Jew, she was a Canaanite. She was the wife of Judah's oldest son, but the man was wicked and the scriptures tell us God killed him. As was the custom she was then given to Judah's second son who was then to have children by her and any children she bore would be considered children of the dead older son (crazy custom but that is how they did it). However, the second son did not want to get her pregnant, he probably liked being the oldest and heir apparent and so took measures to see that she didn't get pregnant. Such behavior, however, displeased God and so He struck this son dead too. Judah began to see a pattern here and did not want to give Tamar to his next and last son for fear he would die too. So he told Tamar to go home to her parents and when the third son was old enough he would send for her and give her to this son too. However, the son grew up but Judah did not send for Tamar.

When Tamar realized that she was not going to be sent for, she dressed as a harlot, which in those days included wearing a veil, and went and sat down beside the road that Judah used to go and come from his home. When Judah saw the veiled harlot he did not recognize her as his daughter-in-law. He offered her a goat for her services. She agreed and they had sex. When Judah went to leave she asked for something to keep until the goat was delivered. He gave her his seal and his rod as security. Judah went his way and when he got to his herd he sent one of his men back with a goat for the prostitute. But the man could not find the harlot. She had taken Judah's security deposit and left.

Some months later Judah was told that Tamar was pregnant. Enraged that his daughter-in-law would fool around he hypocritically ordered her to be taken and stoned to death for her sin. However, Tamar then brought forward Judah's security deposit and he realized what had happened. He spared Tamar, took her as his wife, (one has to wonder about the quality their relationship) and the child born, Phares, is in the direct line of Christ's forefathers.

Generations later the armies of Israel are trying to take the Holy Land over and take the land God had promised them for their nation. The first city that they attacked after crossing into what would one day be Israel was Jericho. Before attacking Jericho, however, they sent some spies into the city to scope it out. These spies stayed in home of Rahab the Harlot. Whether they availed themselves of her services, the scriptures do not tell us.

Rahab is not dumb and realizes that these men are Israelite spies, but she does not turn them over to the local police, she lies to city officials about them, and hides and protects them when city authorities come looking for the spies. In return she asks them to protect her and her family when Jericho is attacked. The spies promise that she and hers will be spared. They are good to their word, Rahab and her family a spared..

Later Rahab is taken to wife by Salmon a descendant of Phares.

Rahab and Salmon have a son Boaz. He lives in Bethlehem where Christ would later be born. A cousin of his takes a non-Jewish wife. Her name is Ruth. Her story is one of the more famous ones in the Bible and you will be familiar with it. The cousin dies, and Ruth ends up married to Boaz and the two of them are King David's great grandparents.

I bring this all to your attention for I know not why, other than I feel led to include it, I am not sure of the lesson to be had here. All three women are non Jews yet end up in the linage of Christ. It is interesting that two other women are mentioned in other books of the New Testament as being in Chirst's line. His mother Mary, is of course one of them. The other is Bathsheba, who may or may not have been Jewish herself. I am inclined to believe she wasn't. She was married to a Hittite soldier. She, of course is the woman who David spotted bathing and lusting after her, sent for her and later had her husband killed so he could take her for himself. Thus three of the five women that we know of in Christ's line are women that would have been looked down on by the Jews of Christ's day. Three were "fallen" women (who probably later took advantage of the gospel and became godly women). Why they find their way into the scriptures where the others (likely good God fearing Jewish women) do not is a mystery to me. I am sure there is a lesson to be had here, I am just in the dark as to what it is.

34 Which was *the son* of Jacob, which was *the son* of Isaac, which was *the son* of Abraham, which was *the son* of Thara, which was *the son* of Nachor,

35 Which was *the son* of Saruch, which was *the son* of Ragau, which was *the son* of Phalec, which was *the son* of Heber, which was *the son* of Sala,

36 Which was *the son* of Cainan, which was *the son* of Arphaxad,

which was *the son* of Sem, which was *the son* of Noe, which was *the son* of Lamech,

37 Which was *the son* of Mathusala, which was *the son* of Enoch, which was *the son* of Jared, which was *the son* of Maleleel, which was *the son* of Cainan,

38 Which was *the son* of Enos, which was *the son* of Seth, which was *the son* of Adam, which was *the son* of God.

Chapter 4

1 AND Jesus being full of the Holy Ghost returned from Jordan, and was led by the Spirit into the wilderness,
2 **Being forty days tempted of the devil**. And in those days he did eat nothing: and when they were ended, he afterward hungered.

Numbers in the Bible often have their own meaning. That Christ was tempted forty days and not thirty nine or forty one is no accident. Forty is the number of trial, hence the Children Of Israel wondered in the Wilderness forty years. Do a word search through the Bible sometime and see how often the number forty appears and how often it has to do with some sort of trial. In another instance, Samuel said God did not want Israel to have a king but the people kept asking for one. Finally Heavenly Father gave in to their desires. Interestingly, the first three kings, Saul, David, and Solomon all reigned for forty years each. One must be careful of any numbers found in the scriptures. They may be the literal number of whatever is in question, or they may have a numerological meaning that the author is attempting to get across.

3 And the devil said unto him, If thou be the Son of God, command this stone that it be made bread.
4 And Jesus answered him, saying, It is written, That man shall not live by bread alone, but by every word of God.
5 And the devil, taking him up into an high mountain, shewed unto him all the kingdoms of the world in a moment of time.
6 And the devil said unto him, **All this power will I give thee, and the glory of them: for that is delivered unto me; and to whomsoever I**

will I give it.
7 If thou therefore wilt worship me, all shall be thine.

Satan is a liar, the words highlighted above being cases in point. Those foolish enough to try and deal with him will find that out quickly. Satan does not control who the world's rulers are. Many, if not most are bad, but this is the result of natural human failings. If Satan were really picking our rulers we would be even worse off.

8 And Jesus answered and said unto him, Get thee behind me, Satan: for it is written, Thou shalt worship the Lord thy God, and him only shalt thou serve.
9 And he brought him to Jerusalem, and set him on a pinnacle of the temple, and said unto him, If thou be the Son of God, cast thyself down from hence:
10 For it is written, He shall give his angels charge over thee, to keep thee:
11 And in *their* hands they shall bear thee up, lest at any time thou dash thy foot against a stone.
12 And Jesus answering said unto him, It is said, Thou shalt not tempt the Lord thy God.
13 And when the devil had ended all the temptation, he departed from him for a season.
14 ¶ And Jesus returned in the power of the Spirit into Galilee: and there went out a fame of him through all the region round about.
15 And he taught in their synagogues, **being glorified of all.**

The honeymoon won't last long. The truth hurts, and those hurt will often be offended, and the offended are likely to lash out. There once was an old man who went to church and heard a sermon that hit too close to home. He was offended by the sermon and told the pastor, "You've done laid off preaching and gone to meddling." A lot of those who heard Christ's message took that same attitude.

16 ¶ And he came to Nazareth, where he had been brought up: and, as his custom was, he went into the synagogue on the sabbath day, and **stood up for to read**.

I believe this is a voluntary thing, this standing to read. Here we see Christ setting things up to begin his ministry.

17 **And there was delivered unto him the book of the prophet Esaias. And when he had opened the book, he found the place where it was written,**
18 **The Spirit of the Lord** *is* **upon me, because he hath anointed me to preach the gospel to the poor; he hath sent me to heal the brokenhearted, to preach deliverance to the captives, and recovering of sight to the blind, to set at liberty them that are bruised,**
19 **To preach the acceptable year of the Lord.**
20 **And he closed the book, and he gave** *it* **again to the minister, and sat down. And the eyes of all them that were in the synagogue were fastened on him.**
21 **And he began to say unto them, This day is this scripture fulfilled in your ears.**

So then, He stood to read, the scroll is passed to Him and Christ looks for this specific passage from Old Testament to read and to at the same time set the tone for His ministry. This is not happenstance. The Old Testament, which contained the only scriptures available at that time, is full of thunderous preachments against sin and pronouncements of death, destruction, and doom. In fact, such negativity is the norm, for Old Testament prophets. They welded the stick much more than they offered the carrot in their attempts to keep the Israelites on the straight and narrow. Yet our Savior, in what can be thought of as his keynote address, the one that starts him on his ministry finds a passage that sets a different tone from what can be seen as a scriptural norm for His day and age.

A hell and damnation preacher would not likely select that passage as the text for his sermon, but Christ did. I think it speaks to the misdirection of many of today's churches that their pastors feel they have to scare the people of their congregation into obedience. I will have to grant, it is a method of conversion. I can't think of the reference, but Paul says words to the effect that some are won over by being frightened into conversion and others won over by being loved into conversion. However, I think fire and brimstone should be used as a last resort, and not the method of choice.

Still, I guess it has it place. When Jonathan Edwards, the famous preacher in the early American colonies gave his renown sermon "Sinners in the Hands of an Angry God," it is said people were crying out and holding on to the pews in fear they would fall into the hands of an angry god.

So then, frightening followers was and still is a common form of intimidation used by churches to get and keep their flocks in line.

Oh, but what a contrast Jesus Christ has to offer. In His first public pronouncement He says He has a different message, and if I am not mistaken he is saying He has a different audience too. Picture, if you will, the scene Luke sets for us here. Jesus is in the established church of His day. Who then is his audience? There were many sects of Jews at the time, not unlike our different denominations of today. However there was one big difference, the various sects did not each have their own meetinghouse and churches. In Christ's time there was just one temple in Jerusalem for all of Jews, and a village would have just one synagogue for them to meet in on the Sabbath. So when Jesus stood up to read, the congregation in front of Him would be filled with the "Holier Than Thou" types that plagued His entire ministry. Listening to him in the congregation would be Pharisees, Sadducees, lawyers, scribes, etc.

Having said who was there listening, we now have to ask who wasn't there listening to him? How about the people He said he was going to minister too? It starts with the poor. Jesus had just said he was going to preach to the poor. If they were there, if there was any room for them at all, it would be in the back, and out of sight. The rich and powerful got the front row seats in church just as they did in the rest of life. James, in his epistle chides the early church for falling back into this same system of honoring the rich over the poor. So, I do not think many poor would be in attendance. Would you go to a church that told you to sit in the back and be as inconspicuous as possible? Doubtful.

How about the brokenhearted? Would they be there? Well if you were feeling down and out, and life was treating you poorly would you go to church hopping to hear a good old hell and damnation sermon? After all, there is nothing like a good fire and brimstone sermon to restore your good feelings. Right? Wrong! I doubt seriously that people weighted down and sorrowing would be in Christ's congregation that day. No I think the brokenhearted stayed home too.

How about the captives? In that passage Christ quoted he says he is going to deliver the captives. I am not sure who the "captives" are, but I would guess He speaks of those caught up in sin and addicted to it, living degenerate lives. Again someone not very likely to be in church that day and listening when Christ said he was going to deliver them from the power of the sin that currently held them captive.

How about the blind? Christ says he is going to help them

recover their ability to see. In Jesus day sickness was seen as a punishment for sin. If you were blind it was because you or maybe your parents had done some terrible sin and this malady, this blindness, you were stricken with, it was a punishment for that sin. So then, a blind person in the synagogue would be seen like the proverbial whore in church, and not welcome. Not many people go where they are not welcome, and I doubt many blind were there to hear Christ's reading of the scriptures.

How about the bruised. Here again, I do not know for sure whom the scriptures are speaking of when the word "bruised" is used. Obviously, we are again speaking of someone with troubles. Not likely the self satisfied and sanctimonious people most apt to have heard Christ speak that day.

So then it would appear that Christ is telling those who heard him that morning that He has a ministry, but it is not with them. He will be taking his message to a different group. His gospel is for those left out by the church of His day. His gospel is for those that the "religious people" distain. In essences he is telling them goodbye. He is telling them his ministry is with others, others that should be here, but aren't. I believe He is telling those hearing him that morning, "You keep these poor, brokenhearted, captives away, holding them at arms distance. But instead of pushing them away, I am going to embrace them."

I wrote the above some time ago. I still believe what I said but I was bothered by preaching **recovering of sight to the blind.** *What I said about the blind is true but I was bothered by its inclusion in the list Christ read. It just didn't seem to fit, and how do you preach recovery to them.*

If you have ever taken an IQ test you will remember one of their favorite ways of testing a person is to give them a list of words and ask

*which one does not belong. The list might be Horse, Dog , Rat, Bird.
Bird does not belong. The first three are mammals, they are four
legged, walk about, and have fir. A bird is two legged, has feathers, and
flies. With the list that Jesus read we have Poor, Brokenhearted,
Captives, Blind, and Bruised. All are bad, but Blind is different from the
others. It is a physical malady. The rest are conditions. This bothered
me and I pondered it a lot.*

*Recently I was preparing to visit a family that I minister to. I
have three such families that I visit monthly, teach a lesson too, and
help out in any way I can. As I prepared that day to go out and teach I
found that our family's copy of The Ensign (the church's magazine with
good articles and teaching materials) was missing. My wife had taken it
with her while she went to minister, like me, to one of the ladies she was
assigned to watch over. With no teaching material ready to hand I had
to come up with a lesson on my own. I found myself led to a passage in
Second Peter that is God's success formula for us. It would make a
good lesson for my family. It reads as follows:*

**5 And beside this, giving all diligence, add to your faith virtue; and
to virtue knowledge;**

**6 And to knowledge temperance; and to temperance patience; and
to patience godliness;**

**7 And to godliness brotherly kindness; and to brotherly kindness
charity.**

**8 For if these things be in you, and abound, they make you that ye
shall neither be barren nor unfruitful in the knowledge of our Lord
Jesus Christ.**

**9 But he that lacketh these things is blind, and cannot see afar off,
and hath forgotten that he was purged from his old sins.**

Do the things listed and Peter says and you will be a fruitful Christian. However, he says, if we lack these qualities we are blind, and have forgotten we were purged from our old sins. There it was. My troubles about preaching to the blind were solved. The passage that Christ read in the synagogue was not referring to those who were physically blind, He was referring to those who have fallen into inactivity, and left the church. Christ will be preaching to them, helping them find their way back.

Also it should be noted that Christ did not follow what I would say is the norm in setting up a new religion. You want to start a new church today you need some new doctrine. Something to set you and any followers you attract apart from the rest. This is almost always some belief you will pedal. The more plausible yet different your new doctrine is the more likely you are to attract followers. But Christ did not choose that path. Instead he talks not of what Heavenly Father is made of, or how far you can walk on the Sabbath, or original sin, or predestination, or all those other nuances of belief that separate His churches today.

For example, how often I have heard of people almost ready to fight over whether the bread and drink taken during the sacrament actually become Christ's body and blood, or are the body and blood sort of hovering over the elements, or maybe it is all symbolic. There are people out there of each opinion and they can get quite upset with you if you do not agree with them.

*The Father of the Protestant Reformation, Luther, believed the bread and wine became the actual body and blood of Christ. When called before a tribunal to defend his views he pounded the table and said in Latin **hoc est corpus meum.** That translates as "this is my body," and is a quote of Christ's words at the Last Supper. He believed that the elements of the sacrament actually became Christ's body and blood. Interestingly, magicians have picked up the phrase and changed it to*

"Hocus Pocus" which they say when changing something into something else, like a scarf into a white rabbit, etc.

How baptism is performed is another way the church is divided. Is it done by sprinkling, pouring, or immersing? There are churches that are identical in their beliefs except they part company over the above question. Adherents of one form of baptism shunning those that hold to another. Sad. I think that someone that holds to the correct form of baptism, but does not live a spiritual life, will find it harder to gain entrance to heaven than someone who was baptized wrong but lives a Christ like life.

But Christ does not announce a new catechism, a new system of beliefs, some new doctrine. He announces that he is going to make the lives of the down and out people in his society better. He is going to preach not some crazy new idea, he going to preach deliverance, recovery of sight, and liberty. His is not a church based on a system of beliefs. His is a church of regeneration, of spirituality, and love. I can never seem to get away from the Apostle Paul's resolve when going to Corinth to start a new church to not get caught up in intellectual arguments. Instead he says, "I determined to know nothing among you except Jesus Christ and him crucified." Paul was there to talk of the atonement and the life altering changes that result from it. He was not going there to set their minds right, he was there to set lives right. And it should be noted that following that resolve Paul enjoyed his greatest success as a missionary, starting his largest church.

Here is an interesting story. In the early 1800's a man, who had spoken to a Mormon Missionary, wrote Joseph Smith, the Prophet, and said, "I have wished to know the truth, and consider myself [ready] to receive it come from where it may come. I now wish to know through you the laws and regulations of your church. What is required of its members? How much, if a man of property, must he contribute annually for its support. In short what is required to constitute good membership?"

Joseph Smith replied: "In answer I would remark that it is required of all men to have faith in the Lord Jesus Christ and to repent of their sins and be baptized (by one in authority) in the Name of Jesus Christ for the remission of sins and to have hands laid on them for the gift of the Holy Ghost to constitute a member of the Church of Jesus Christ of Latter Day Saints...

Respecting how much a man of property shall give annually, we have no special instruction to give. He is to feed the hungry, to clothe the naked, to provide for the widow, to dry up the tear of the orphan, to comfort the afflicted, whether in this church or any other or in no church at all, wherever he finds them. To believe and obey all that God has revealed, does reveal, or will reveal, to do good to all men."

Doesn't that sound more like what Christ said He was about than the mumbo jumbo we get from the run of the mill churches today. Instead of doctrines and rules, Joseph talks of lifestyle much as Christ did.

My studies of the life of Joseph Smith have shown him to be a man who loved the study of doctrine. He ventured into it many times, but it was not at the core of his life. For him it was an avocation, something of interest, even intense interest, but not anywhere near the consequence of how a person lived their life and ministered to others

I think we are getting to the core of the truth, or close to it. Jesus says He is going to minister to the poor, brokenhearted, captives, blind, and bruised. If that is the case then those are the persons who we should find in the congregation of His church. If you walk in on a Sunday morning and find a crowd of self-righteous, doctrinal purests, with a bunch of rules they want you to follow you have not come to the right spot. Instead Christ's church will be filled with the poor, brokenhearted, captives, blind, and bruised. At least there will be a lot of those there seeking to make their lives better. The rest of the congregation will be made up of those who, through the power of the gospel in their lives, have escaped those conditions and now are living happy righteous lives.

22 And all bare him witness, and wondered at the gracious words which proceeded out of his mouth. And they said, Is not this Joseph's son?

It would seem the congregation that He spoke to that morning were somewhat dumbfounded. That would change over time, as we shall see. But at first they are content to marvel that Joseph's son has turned out so eloquent.

23 And he said unto them, Ye will surely say unto me this proverb, Physician, heal thyself: **whatsoever we have heard done in Capernaum, do also here in thy country.**

They had heard of miracles done elsewhere, and wanted him to put on a show for them.

24 And he said, **Verily I say unto you, No prophet is accepted in his own country.**

I think He is telling them they do not understand. I think he is saying that because they saw Him grow up, they just think it is quaint that a boy from their midst make claims like Jesus just did. They saw him play as a youth. They saw him work in his dad's carpenter shop. Now he is a man and telling them He has great plans to minister to the down and out, and that He would go so far as to say that He was the fulfillment of scriptures. It is hard for them to reconcile this new "ministry" with the man who was just one of them for so many years.

25 **But I tell you of a truth, many widows were in Israel in the days of Elias, when the heaven was shut up three years and six months, when great famine was throughout all the land;**

26 **But unto none of them was Elias sent, save unto Sarepta, *a city* of Sidon, unto a woman *that was* a widow.**

27 **And many lepers were in Israel in the time of Eliseus the prophet; and none of them was cleansed, saving Naaman the Syrian.**

28 **And all they in the synagogue, when they heard these things, were filled with wrath,**

Now he has gotten them mad. Like so many in this world today, these, his people, were bigots and racists. He enrages them by reminding them of a couple instances where worthy Jewish people were by passed by Heavenly Father and miracles were performed for the benefit of gentiles instead. Now Christ is not saying He will go to the gentiles, but I think He is telling them that Nazareth will not be where He works His miracles. This upsets them, and does so probably on two levels, first that He says "no" to their request for miracles, and second His reminding them that Heavenly Father has bypassed Israel in the past, something they could take no joy in, not with their attitude towards non Jewish people.

Humans are usually content in their racist attitudes. I think it takes a conscious effort to overcome them. They seem to be the norm, and a cosmopolitan attitude the exception. Now I will admit, times are changing, and our youth seem much less race conscious than their elders. But it is still a problem. And where it is not a racial prejudice we have to deal with it is a national pride/prejudice issue we have to overcome. We look down our noses at others for either racial or cultural pride reasons, maybe both. But the fact remains, for whatever reason, we think we are superior to others. This is especially true in politics today. If anyone finds something admirable in another race or people, then it is seen as a putdown of our own society by those on the right wing of politics. These people forget that our country is a melting pot. What we have, we have gotten from others. That is not a process that has ceased to be operative. As much as some people seem to dislike it, and want to stop the clock, and freeze things just as the are (or worse still, go back to the good old days) that is not the dynamic that is in operation. We are growing and changing, sometimes for the worse, but mostly for the better.

29 And rose up, and thrust him out of the city, and led him unto the brow of the hill whereon their city was built, that they might cast him down headlong
30 But he passing through the midst of them went his way,

It would seem that some sort of miracle took place here. A mob is a terrible thing, and to just pass through them would take some higher power at work. LDS people in particular know the truth of that statement. Murdered and run off their lands in Missouri, Persequted in New York, Ohio, and Utah, the church has known much affliction. However, Heavenly Father has never abandon His people, nor will he.

31 And came down to Capernaum, a city of Galilee, and taught them on the Sabbath days.
32 And they were astonished at his doctrine: **for his word was with power.**

This is not referring to oratorical skill. The Holy Spirit can speed words to a person's heart in ways a neat turn of phrase never could. I heard an apocryphal tale of a man who is greeting his pastor at the churches door at the end of Sunday services. When asked how he liked the sermon, he told the pastor that he didn't care much for it because: "he had laid off preaching and gone to meddling." How true. We all like a sermon or talk in church that makes us feel comfortable, but not so much the ones that get down next to where we live and show up our weaknesses. However, making us feel good is not the usual goal of the Holy Spirit. I think we do that well enough on our own. The Spirit instead is there to show us our short comings and how we can do better. In light of what was said about hell and damnation preaching earlier in comments about this chapter, let me say that I see the work of the Holy Spirit not as a frightening entity, but as a coach trying to help us do better.

33 ¶ And in the synagogue there was a man, which had a spirit of an unclean devil, and cried out with a loud voice,

34 **Saying, Let *us* alone; what have we to do with thee, *thou* Jesus of Nazareth? Art thou come to destroy us? I know thee who thou art; the Holy One of God.**

35 And Jesus rebuked him, saying, Hold thy peace, and come out of him. And when the devil had thrown him in the midst, he came out of him, and hurt him not.

36 And they were all amazed, and spake among themselves, saying, What a word *is* this! For with authority and power he commandeth the unclean spirits, and they come out.

37 And the fame of him went out into every place of the country round about.

James, in his epistle says the devils believe and tremble. Here is an example. This demon recognizes Christ for who and what he is. Many of the men and women around Jesus, his supposed followers, doubted him and/or left Him, but not this minion of Lucifer. This unclean spirit believed all the doctrine, had sure faith that Christ was the Holy One of God, but it would not save him/her. Salvation was no longer open to the demons. All this spirit's faith did it not one bit of good as pertains to its ultimate destination. This demon probably had a PhD in doctrine, but believing all the intellectual nuances didn't help it. So I think there's an

*important lesson to learn here. Our salvation hinges on more than just
a lot of knowledge. Christ said elsewhere you need the faith of a child
to enter His Father's Kingdom. I am sorry but children are not much
good at doctrine and the "deeper things" of the Bible. They understand
simple trust. That is a concept they can get a hold of. And that is all that
Heavenly Father really wants of them or us. He desires a child like trust
in the atoning sacrifice of Jesus for our sins. As Paul makes clear in
one of his epistles: "And Abraham believed God and it was counted
unto him for righteousness." So many Churches take the attitude that a
person must accept their version different doctrines in order to be
"Saved." I do not believe the scriptures would support such an attitude.
A thousand years ago they argued over how many angels could dance
on the head of a pin. Today they argue over how many parts God might
have. I do not think having the right answer to either of those questions,
or to the many other questions that divide Christians will help one get
into heaven. That demon knew all the answers, it did it no good. Simple
faith in Christ, that's all that is needed. As Paul said when he went to
Corinth to preach the gospel, "I determined to know nothing among
you save Jesus Christ and him crucified." That is the simple gospel that
joins Christians, and does not divide them like "doctrine" does.*

38 ¶ And he arose out of the synagogue, and entered into Simon's
house. And Simon's wife's mother was taken with a great fever; and
they besought him for her.
39 **And he stood over her, and rebuked the fever; and it left her:
and immediately she arose and ministered unto them.**

*There's just something about spiritual women, they thrive on serving
others. Jesus said that the first would be last and the last first. This is a
principle that women seem to be able to embrace much more readily
than men.*

In these last two sections that we've commented on we find an emphasis on humility. Christ amazes the throng when he casts out to demon. After such a miracle he would've been welcome in any home in the city. Instead he goes to the home of a common fishermen. Of course, Simon was also his disciple and visiting the man's home would not be unusual. However, the fact remains Christ performs a miracle and afterwards goes to what is probably one of the more humble dwellings in the village. Once there he heals Simon's mother-in-law and she arises from her sick bed and begins serving everyone in the house.

So often churches rely on the pageantry of people marching to the altar in robes and with candles and with inscense burning, or the beauty of a cathedral, or possible the certainty of a ritual to enthrall the masses. That would not seem to be the method employed by Christ.

40 ¶ Now when the sun was setting, all they that had any sick with divers diseases brought them unto him; and he laid his hands on every one of them, and healed them.

41 And devils also came out of many, crying out, and saying, Thou art Christ the Son of God. And he rebuking *them* suffered them not to speak: for they knew that he was Christ.

I'm not sure I really understand why Christ felt the need to shut the demon's mouths. If you read this and similar passages in other Gospels you might possibly come away with the impression that at least at this stage of his ministry Christ was not yet declaring himself to be the Messiah. Possibly he didn't want demons letting the cat out of the bag. Or maybe it's just the demons are wicked and evil beings and Christ doesn't want their witness to his divinity. When I ran for public office, and was elected to the School Board I would not have wanted the endorsement of anybody I vehemently disagreed with. Christ not wanting the demons to speak of Him may be nothing deeper than my experience.

42 And when it was day, he departed and went into a desert place: and the people sought him, and came unto him, and stayed him, that he should not depart from them.

43 And he said unto them, I must preach the kingdom of God to other cities also: for therefore am I sent.

44 And he preached in the synagogues of Galilee.

Chapter 5

1 AND it came to pass, that, as the people pressed upon him to hear the word of God, he stood by the lake of Gennesaret,
2 And saw two ships standing by the lake: but the fishermen were gone out of them, and were washing *their* nets.
3 And he entered into one of the ships, which was Simon's, and prayed him that he would thrust out a little from the land. **And he sat down, and taught the people out of the ship.**

I think that it's interesting that he sat down and then talked to people from a sitting position. The informality of teaching from a sitting position seems to me to say something about the Master's whole attitude. He didn't need a pulpit. He didn't need to be high up somewhere looking down at the people. So often preachers take on what I call the sanctified voice when they're behind the pulpit. They wear fancy vestments to set themselves apart from their people. The purpose of all this is to put us in awe of what they're saying. None of that for Christ, he just sat and taught, and the simple truths he was speaking, they were what that put people in awe of the speaker.

4 Now when he had left speaking, he said unto Simon, Launch out into the deep, and let down your nets for a draught.
5 **And Simon answering said unto him, Master, we have toiled all the night, and have taken nothing: nevertheless at thy word I will let down the net.**

"I'm tired, and it's a waste of time, but you're the boss so I will do what you say." Isn't that what Peter seems to be saying in so many the words? It's not exactly the way one would expect him to address his Messiah. So then does Christ rebuked him for speaking in such a manner? No. What then is the lesson we should be learning here? Might it hark back to the previous passage we discussed, where we saw Christ sitting to teach? I think the answer is yes. I think what we have here is not an example of St. Peter's testiness, but rather the informal relationship between Jesus and his disciples. His manner of teaching, and his relationship with his disciples are both laid back and that is an interesting insight into the type man Jesus was. He created the world, but He doesn't let it go to His head. It just seems to me this is not how most people see Christ acting. I don't think they see Him as some sanctimonious buffoon with his nose in the clouds, but neither do they see him as some one who Peter can mouth off to either. Yet it appears that is just the kind of man He was. The Prophet Joseph Smith was a similar man. He loved to wrestle. He participated in other sports too. In fact, it is possible he participated in some of the earliest baseball games, playing baseball with the youth of Nauvoo, in the early 1840's.

6 And when they had this done, they inclosed a great multitude of fishes: and their net brake.

7 And they beckoned unto *their* partners, which were in the other ship, that they should come and help them. And they came, and filled both the ships, so that they began to sink.

8 **When Simon Peter saw** *it,* **he fell down at Jesus' knees, saying, Depart from me; for I am a sinful man, O Lord.**

In spite of his flippant tone when speaking to the Savior just a few verses prior to this, Peter knows that he and Jesus are two very different people. He knew that Jesus was the man who had the words of life.

9 For he was astonished, and all that were with him, at the draught of the fishes which they had taken:

10 And so *was* also James, and John, the sons of Zebedee, which were partners with Simon. And Jesus said unto Simon, Fear not; from henceforth thou shalt catch men.

11 And when they had brought their ships to land, **they forsook all**, and followed him.

I believe that what happened was they just walked away from their livelihood. They didn't first have a garage sale and put their boat up for sale. They just walked away from everything and followed Jesus. That tells me they were good men, pious men, and worthy men. Church tradition says all of Jesus's apostles, with the exception of John, died for to their faith in Jesus. We too need to forsake things of the world and follow Jesus in service to our fellow man. Ministering to others is more important than money in the bank.

12 ¶ And it came to pass, when he was in a certain city, behold a man full of leprosy: who seeing Jesus fell on *his* face, and besought him, saying, Lord, if thou wilt, thou canst make me clean.

13 And he put forth *his* hand, and touched him, saying, I will: be thou clean. And immediately the leprosy departed from him.

14 And he charged him to tell no man: **but go, and shew thyself to the priest, and offer for thy cleansing, according as Moses commanded, for a testimony unto them.**

Jesus was an observant Jew. He followed the Law and expected others to also. The Old Testament taught that a person who thought they were healed of leprosy was to present themselves to a Priest who would look him/her over and if they agreed that a cure had taken place the priest would declare the person clean and so they could reenter society (lepers were considered unclean and couldn't live with other

15 But so much the more went there a fame abroad of him: and great
multitudes came together to hear, and to be healed by him of their
infirmities.

16 ¶ And he withdrew himself into the wilderness, and prayed.

17 And it came to pass on a certain day, as he was teaching, that there
were Pharisees and doctors of the law sitting by, which were come out
of every town of Galilee, and Judæa, and Jerusalem: and the power of
the Lord was *present* to heal them.

18 ¶ And, behold, men brought in a bed a man which was taken with a
palsy: and they sought *means* to bring him in, and to lay *him* before
him.

19 And when they could not find by what *way* they might bring him in
because of the multitude, they went upon the housetop, and let him
down through the tiling with *his* couch into the midst before Jesus.

20 **And when he saw their faith, he said unto him, Man, thy sins are
forgiven thee.**

21 **And the scribes and the Pharisees began to reason, saying, Who
is this which speaketh blasphemies? Who can forgive sins, but God
alone?**

*The lawyers and Pharisees are not wrong here. God alone can forgive
sins. Their problem is they do not recognize Christ's divinity. They also
do not realize that God can delegate the ability to forgive sins. Later
Jesus tells his disciples that "what they loose on earth will be loosed in
heaven."*

22 But when Jesus perceived their thoughts, he answering said unto
them, What reason ye in your hearts?

23 **Whether is easier, to say, Thy sins be forgiven thee; or to say, Rise up and walk?**

I do not believe that Christ is saying that forgiving sins and healing are the same thing. Nor do I believe that sickness is the result of sin. At another time Christ healed a blind man. Afterwards His disciples came and asked Christ if the man's blindness was the result of his own sin or his parents sin. Christ told them neither had resulted in the man's blindness and that it was so God and His power over sickness could be demonstrated. Having said all that, I do believe that sin can lead to physical problems. A man can get drunk, drive his car while under the influence, get in an accident and have an injury that results in the loss of an arm. He can later repent of what he did, gain forgiveness of his sins and his arm will not be restored (or at least I have not heard of any such healings). Sin can result in physical problems, but it does not follow that physical problems are because of sin. Nor does forgiveness of sins equate with physical health. You can be a healthy sinner or a sick saint, and you can also be a sick sinner or a healthy saint.

The important thing is that you live the right kind of life and do so until the end of your life. In Martin Luther's day a man named Tetzel was selling "indulgences" that were issued by the Catholic Church to raise money for the building of Saint Peter's Cathedral. These indulgences forgave a person's sins. You paid whatever amount they were selling for and you were forgiven. You even received an official written notice of your sins having been forgiven. You could also purchase them for a dead friend or relative. Tetzel was famous for saying the instant your coin clinked in the bottom of his strong box, the person for whom you had purchased the indulgence, their soul flew from purgatory and up to heaven. Luther opposed this and his opposition became the main basis for his leaving the Catholic church and starting Lutheran Church.

Today, we have the doctrine of "once saved, always saved." It is

24 But that ye may know that the Son of man hath power upon earth to forgive sins, (he said unto the sick of the palsy,) I say unto thee, Arise, and take up thy couch, and go into thine house.
25 And immediately he rose up before them, and took up that whereon he lay, and departed to his own house, glorifying God.
26 And they were all amazed, and they glorified God, and were filled with fear, saying, We have seen strange things to day.
27 ¶ And after these things he went forth, and saw a publican, named Levi, sitting at the receipt of custom: and he said unto him, Follow me.
28 **And he left all, rose up, and followed him.**

Like Peter, James, and John, Levi (read Matthew) just dropped everything and followed Christ.

29 And Levi made him a great feast in his own house: and there was a great company of publicans and of others that sat down with them.
30 **But their scribes and Pharisees murmured against his disciples, saying, Why do ye eat and drink with publicans and sinners?**
31 **And Jesus answering said unto them, They that are whole need**

not a physician; but they that are sick.

32 I came not to call the righteous, but sinners to repentance.

I think we have an example here of Christ's sense of humor. He is flattering the scribes and Pharisees. Either they are too dumb to recognize that He is poking fun at them or so caught up in their own self-righteousness that they are forced to agree with Him.

33 ¶ And they said unto him, Why do the disciples of John fast often, and make prayers, and likewise *the disciples* of the Pharisees; but thine eat and drink?

34 And he said unto them, Can ye make the children of the bridechamber fast, while the bridegroom is with them?

35 But the days will come, when the bridegroom shall be taken away from them, and then shall they fast in those days.

36 ¶ And he spake also a parable unto them; No man putteth a piece of a new garment upon an old; if otherwise, then both the new maketh a rent, and the piece that was *taken* out of the new agreeth not with the old.

37 And no man putteth new wine into old bottles; else the new wine will burst the bottles, and be spilled, and the bottles shall perish.

38 But new wine must be put into new bottles; and both are preserved.

39 No man also having drunk old *wine* straightway desireth new: for he saith, The old is better.

Here we see Christ speaking in a parable, a story with a lesson to be learned. That lesson is not always obvious. Christ often spoke in parables because He did not want to come right out and say something. As to the "why" of the secrecy I can't say. I do not know. I guess it was because his listeners were not ready for the truth.

Here I think He is saying that His church, at least as He envisioned it will be new and different. It is not going to be a patch of new cloth on the old Jewish religion. It is not going to be new wine in the old wine skin of Old Testament religious practices. (Luke says bottles, but I believe that is a error in translation. Glass was a luxury in Chirst's time. Wine was typically kept in wine skins.)

Try patching an old piece of cloth with a new piece and the result is a tear. The old will have already shrunk or stretched as much as it is going to. The new piece of cloth will not yet have gone through that process and so it when it does it will tear free of the old. Try putting new wine in an old wine skin and the result is a burst wine skin. The old wine skin will again have already done its stretching. The new wine, however, will not have fermented yet and so when it does the gasses created will burst the old already stretched out wine skin.

Try making Christ's church just another Jewish sect and the result will be a rending of the old cloth or wine skin. This was a lesson Luke knew well for his other book in the New Testament is the Book of Acts, which features the Apostle Paul's struggles to break the church free from its Jewish roots and make it a religion of its own. Christ knew this scission would take place and was alluding to it in the parable above.

Chapter 6

1 **AND it came to pass on the second sabbath after the first, that he went through the corn fields; and his disciples plucked the ears of corn, and did eat, rubbing *them* in *their* hands.**

Another mistranslation here. Corn was a new world food. Europe, Asia, the Holy Land, etc. only learned of it after Columbus. What the disciples are gathering is some grain, most likely heads of wheat. That is why they are rubbing it in their hands, to get off the chaff so they can then eat it. Corn you shuck, wheat you rub.

2 **And certain of the Pharisees said unto them, Why do ye that which is not lawful to do on the sabbath days?**
3 **And Jesus answering them said, Have ye not read so much as this, what David did, when himself was an hungred, and they which were with him;**
4 **How he went into the house of God, and did take and eat the shewbread, and gave also to them that were with him; which it is not lawful to eat but for the priests alone?**
5 **And he said unto them, That the Son of man is Lord also of the sabbath.**

This is the first of many run ins that Christ will have with Jewish leaders over Sabbath day practices. When the law was given to Moses working on the Sabbath was punishable by death. By Christ's time killing Sabbath breakers was not common if practiced at all, however, just what was allowed on the Sabbath and what wasn't had become quite involved. Over the twelve to fourteen hundred years that followed Moses receiving the law, rabbis had been busy interpreting it. At their hands "Work" took on many new meanings. You could walk from your home but only about 1300 feet, any more was Sabbath breaking. You could warm food, but you could not cook it. The list goes on and on. In this case, by Jewish custom it was legal for someone passing by a field to help themselves to a handful of grain, but only six days a week, not if it was the Sabbath. Picking even just a handful of grain on the Sabbath was "working."

Seeing Christ's disciples "working" on the Sabbath outraged the Pharisees. Like so many religious hypocrites today, they were very legalistic. They followed the letter of law, but ignore its spirit.

6 And it came to pass also on another sabbath, that he entered into the synagogue and taught: and there was a man whose right hand was withered.
7 And the scribes and Pharisees watched him, whether he would heal on the sabbath day; that they might find an accusation against him.
8 But he knew their thoughts, and said to the man which had the withered hand, Rise up, and stand forth in the midst. And he arose and stood forth.
9 Then said Jesus unto them, I will ask you one thing; Is it lawful on the sabbath days to do good, or to do evil? to save life, or to destroy it?
10 And looking round about upon them all, he said unto the man,

Stretch forth thy hand. And he did so: and his hand was restored whole as the other.

11 And they were filled with madness; and communed one with another what they might do to Jesus.

More of the same from the Pharisees. I do not understand people like this. Picture the scene above as Luke relates it. It is the Sabbath, everyone is in church (synagogue) to worship God. A man with a withered hand is in the congregation. The Pharisees are not worshiping they are watching Christ to see what he will do about the man with the bad hand. Apparently "healing" was not on the list of approved activities for the Sabbath and therefore to do so would be "working" and a sin. Christ knows their thoughts so he asks them if it is legal to do good or evil on the Sabbath? They are trapped. If they say the Sabbath is for doing good then healing the man would be ok. Of course they can't say the Sabbath is for evil. So, seeing the trap, they answer nothing. Christ then heals the man.

Note it says that as a result of this confrontation the Pharisees get together and plot with each other about how to deal with Christ. Instead of being overjoyed for the lucky man who had his hand healed they are angry at Christ. It has been my observation that just such a reaction can be looked for today from the doctrinaire. They can't share the joy of someone who "gets religion" unless that getting is in the right church with the right interpretation of some doctrine they hold dear. To them the turning around of a life is of less importance than keeping faith with some idea or teaching. That is not the gospel that was taught by Christ. His gospel is one of redemption through faith, and then living a life worthy of that redemption. "Your sins are forgiven thee, go now and sin no more." That's it. All the other trappings of religion are just that, trappings.

The Apostle James said pure religion is to visit the widows and orphans. He didn't mention getting a PhD in systematic theology. He didn't mention it on purpose, because it has nothing to do with pure religion. Sunday services and involvement in church programs can help a person either find Christ or to stay on the straight and narrow path. They are a good thing. But they are not salvation. Salvation is faith in Christ's atoning sacrifice, and then enduring to the end. All the legalisms that churches try to attach, beliefs they try to make part of salvation don't help anybody find heaven, they are a hindrance, a load too heavy for many to carry, and instead of helping people to heaven, they cause many to stumble and never make it.

12 And it came to pass in those days, that he went out into a mountain to pray, **and continued all night in prayer to God.**

I wonder what it would be like to have an all-night prayer meetings. My prayers are usually short and to the point. Christ did instruct that they be thus elsewhere in the scriptures, but it would seem that while short is good, long has a place too.

13 ¶ And when it was day, he called *unto him* his disciples: and **of them he chose twelve, whom also he named apostles;**
14 Simon, (whom he also named Peter,) and Andrew his brother, James and John, Philip and Bartholomew,
15 Matthew and Thomas, James the *son* of Alphæus, and Simon called Zelotes,
16 And Judas *the brother* of James, and Judas Iscariot, which also was the traitor.

Why twelve and not ten or thirteen or some other number? I am not sure, but numbers have significance in the scriptures. Forty a favorite of Old Testament authors to signify a trial or judgment. Others have other meanings. So twelve is no accident, or just happened to be the number of top disciples. It has a meaning. Today that number is continued in the quorum of the twelve apostles in running the church.

17 ¶ And he came down with them, and stood in the plain, and the company of his disciples, and a great multitude of people out of all Judæa and Jerusalem, and from the sea coast of Tyre and Sidon, which came to hear him, and to be healed of their diseases;
18 And they that were vexed with unclean spirits: and they were healed.
19 **And the whole multitude sought to touch him: for there went virtue out of him, and healed *them* all.**

Elsewhere in the gospels we read of a woman who came up behind Christ and touched him, and virtue went out of him and healed her. She no doubt had heard that just touching Christ would heal her. Others were aware that healing could take place in this manner as is illustrated above. I am not sure just what we are seeing happen here. That Christ consciously healed the sick and afflicted we know. In these instances, however, it is just the faith of the receiver that seems to be at work. Christ has an over abundance of healing virtue, the sick has faith in that virtue and exercises the faith by touching Christ and healing results.

I am thinking this may be a source of the Roman Catholic practice of praying to saints, who they believe also have a overabundance of virtue, and may be persuaded through a believers prayers to expend some of that virtue on their behalf. If this is the source of the Catholic belief, you can see how it makes some sense.

20 ¶ And he lifted up his eyes on his disciples, and said, Blessed *be ye* poor: for yours is the kingdom of God.
21 Blessed *are ye* that hunger now: for ye shall be filled. Blessed *are ye* that weep now: for ye shall laugh.
22 **Blessed are ye, when men shall hate you, and when they shall**

separate you *from their company,* and shall reproach *you,* and cast out your name as evil, for the Son of man's sake.

Sadly, such treatment is happening more and more in the world. A hundred years ago things were going well for "Christanity" and many thought that thousand year reign of Christ over the earth was about to begin. No more. Christians are once again being persecuted throughout the world for political, and religious reasons. At least those who are suffering can call themselves blessed.

23 Rejoice ye in that day, and leap for joy: for, behold, your reward *is* great in heaven: for in the like manner did their fathers unto the prophets.
24 But woe unto you that are rich! for ye have received your consolation.
25 Woe unto you that are full! for ye shall hunger. Woe unto you that laugh now! for ye shall mourn and weep.
26 **Woe unto you, when all men shall speak well of you! for so did their fathers to the false prophets.**
27 **¶ But I say unto you which hear, Love your enemies, do good to them which hate you,**
28 **Bless them that curse you, and pray for them which despitefully use you.**
29 **And unto him that smiteth thee on the *one* cheek offer also the other; and him that taketh away thy cloak forbid not *to take thy* coat also.**
30 **Give to every man that asketh of thee; and of him that taketh away thy goods ask *them* not again.**
31 **And as ye would that men should do to you, do ye also to them likewise.**

I hate to keep repeating myself, but you will notice above that Christ lays out some pretty hard standards for us to keep to after becoming his followers. But not one of these standards is doctrinaire. He does not lay down a system of beliefs. He does not give us a catechism. Instead he offers up a lifestyle, not an easy lifestyle either. Love, turn the other cheek, and give, these are the essence of his church. Too many people today equate doctrinal purity with spiritual purity. They are not the same. One is unimportant and the other is everything.

How many times has Satan driven a wedge between two spiritual followers of Christ over some petty interpretation of scripture? Good people have died, killed by other good people over ideas about the sacrament. Does the host become the body of Christ or is it just a symbol? Does that wine turn into blood? Get the answer wrong five hundred years ago and you could go the stake. Jesus said, "Do this in remembrance of me." It is a time to celebrate his death for us, not an occasion or reason for dealing out death ourselves. You might say that is too extreme. The Church has grown out of those sorts of passions. And you would be right. We don't kill over doctrine anymore, but we sure do let it keep us separate. We still let unimportant ideas keep us apart. ***"By this shall all men know ye are my disciples, that ye love one another."*** *How much love is there between Catholics and Protestants and Mormons and Orthodox and etc. Very little I am afraid.*

32 For if ye love them which love you, what thank have ye? for sinners also love those that love them.

33 And if ye do good to them which do good to you, what thank have ye? for sinners also do even the same.

34 And if ye lend *to them* of whom ye hope to receive, what thank have ye? for sinners also lend to sinners, to receive as much again.

35 But love ye your enemies, and do good, and lend, hoping for nothing again; and your reward shall be great, and ye shall be the children of the Highest: for he is kind unto the unthankful and *to* the evil.

**36 Be ye therefore merciful, as your Father also is merciful.
37 Judge not, and ye shall not be judged: condemn not, and ye shall
not be condemned: forgive, and ye shall be forgiven:**

*The above passage puts me in mind of my favorite Bible verse.
Micah 6:8 which says:* **He hath shewed thee, O man, what is good;
and what doth the LORD require of thee, but to do justly, and to love
mercy, and to walk humbly with thy God?**

**38 Give, and it shall be given unto you; good measure, pressed
down, and shaken together, and running over, shall men give into
your bosom. For with the same measure that ye mete withal it shall
be measured to you again.**

*There are some today that think it is Godly to be rich. The
Puritans who came to America felt the same and that belief became the
under pinning of the American Work Ethic. Work hard and you can get
ahead. It is still this nation's dream. I do not think Christ would agree,
however. He said it is harder for a rich man to go to heaven than for a
camel to get through the eye of a needle. Others, however, read this
verse and think Christ is giving out instructions on how to have
Prosperity here on earth. Give and ye shall receive.*

*I think Christ may be taking the long view. I believe there are
degrees in Heaven. How you treat your fellow man here on earth will in
much part determine your level of reward in heaven. I do not believe
Salvation is a pass/fail test for us. A death bed conversion may get you
through the Pearly Gates but will not get you the same reward as
Zechariahs and Elizabeth of whom we read in the first chapter, who
were "blameless" before God and who spent there lives in serving Him.
I will say, that I also believe (due to Latter Day revelations) God's
kingdom does not have a caste system either. You are not locked into a
level of reward when you arrive. You can move up. Peter may hand you*

a small harp as he passes you through the Pearly Gates, but that does not mean you cannot work you way up to First Violin in the Heavenly Orchestra.

39 And he spake a parable unto them, Can the blind lead the blind? Shall they not both fall into the ditch?
40 The disciple is not above his master: but every one that is perfect shall be as his master.
41 And why beholdest thou the mote that is in thy brother's eye, but perceivest not the beam that is in thine own eye?
42 Either how canst thou say to thy brother, Brother, let me pull out the mote that is in thine eye, when thou thyself beholdest not the beam that is in thine own eye? Thou hypocrite, cast out first the beam out of thine own eye, and then shalt thou see clearly to pull out the mote that is in thy brother's eye.

Notice Christ does not say we are not to help out our brother who has a problem (mote in the eye), he just says get your own self into good condition first. Don't worry about others foibles, get your own life in order. Once you have accomplished that you will be good enough to help our your fellow men/women.

43 For a good tree bringeth not forth corrupt fruit; neither doth a corrupt tree bring forth good fruit.
44 For every tree is known by his own fruit. For of thorns men do not gather figs, nor of a bramble bush gather they grapes.
45 A good man out of the good treasure of his heart bringeth forth that which is good; and an evil man out of the evil treasure of his heart bringeth forth that which is evil: for of the abundance of the heart his mouth speaketh.

46 ¶ And why call ye me, Lord, Lord, and do not the things which I say?

No commentary is needed to understand this verse.

47 Whosoever cometh to me, and heareth my sayings, and doeth them, I will shew you to whom he is like:
48 He is like a man which built an house, and digged deep, and laid the foundation on a rock: and when the flood arose, the stream beat vehemently upon that house, and could not shake it: for it was founded upon a rock.
49 But he that heareth, and doeth not, is like a man that without a foundation built an house upon the earth; against which the stream did beat vehemently, and immediately it fell; and the ruin of that house was great.

When this is taken in conjunction with verse 46 we see that Christ's teachings are the foundation we need to build our lives and families on.

Chapter 7

1 Now when he had ended all his sayings in the audience of the people, he entered into Capernaum.

2 And a certain centurion's servant, who was dear unto him, was sick, and ready to die.

3 And when he heard of Jesus, he sent unto him the elders of the Jews, beseeching him that he would come and heal his servant.

4 And when they came to Jesus, they besought him instantly, saying, That he was worthy for whom he should do this:

5 For he loveth our nation, and he hath built us a synagogue.

6 Then Jesus went with them. And when he was now not far from the house, the centurion sent friends to him, saying unto him, Lord, trouble not thyself: for I am not worthy that thou shouldest enter under my roof:

7 Wherefore neither thought I myself worthy to come unto thee: **but say in a word, and my servant shall be healed.**

8 **For I also am a man set under authority, having under me soldiers, and I say unto one, Go, and he goeth; and to another, Come, and he cometh; and to my servant, Do this, and he doeth it.**

9 **When Jesus heard these things, he marvelled at him, and turned him about, and said unto the people that followed him, I say unto you, I have not found so great faith, no, not in Israel.**

This is an illustration of faith. So often we need more than simple faith. Sight, touch, or feel become necessary for us to believe. Yet with Heavenly Father, just a word is enough. A child stands up on a couch and says "Daddy, catch me." And then launches themselves into the air without a second thought. The child has faith his daddy's arms will find him before the floor comes up to smack him. That is the type of faith that Jesus wants to see. He doesn't always get it. In fact He probably rarely gets that level of faith. It is a good thing for us that He doesn't require it. Just faith the size of a mustard seed can move mountains. What then can be accomplished if we have faith like that exhibited by the centurion.

10 And they that were sent, returning to the house, found the servant whole that had been sick.

11 And it came to pass the day after, that he went into a city called Nain; and many of his disciples went with him, and much people.

12 Now when he came nigh to the gate of the city, behold, there was a dead man carried out, the only son of his mother, and she was a widow: and much people of the city was with her.

13 And when the Lord saw her, he had compassion on her, and said unto her, Weep not.

14 And he came and touched the bier: and they that bare him stood still. And he said, Young man, I say unto thee, Arise.

15 And he that was dead sat up, and began to speak. And he delivered him to his mother.

I think it is interesting that Jesus' compassion is directed towards the widow who has lost her only son instead of the son who has died. In my human fashion I find myself feeling sorry for the dead man instead. I see the resurrection as being something good for him. He's alive again. But Christ is thinking of the mother, at least primarily. Maybe the dead son was enjoying paradise and then was suddenly called back. He may not have been happy about that. Christ understanding all, sees the mother as the one in most need of help and He offers it.

I personally do not believe in these near death experiences we read of. But almost invariably they make out the next world as superior to this one. Joseph Smith taught that there are three levels in heaven and that if people knew how wonderful even the lowest one is, they would be committing suicide to get there.

16 And there came a fear on all: and they glorified God, saying, That a great prophet is risen up among us; and, That God hath visited his people.

We should not find it surprising that Christ raising a man from the dead was greeted with fear. People fear what they do not understand. A true man of God often finds that others fear him too. They see something there that they wish for but don't think they can obtain. They fear a person of such power that they can turn away form all else and embrace godliness.

17 And this rumour of him went forth throughout all Judaea, and throughout all the region round about.
18 And the disciples of John shewed him of all these things.
19 And **John calling unto him two of his disciples sent them to Jesus, saying, Art thou he that should come? or look we for another?**

Jesus and John were 2ⁿᵈ cousins; their mothers were 1ˢᵗ cousins and knew each other. Elizabeth and Mary both knew Christ's roll to play.

In fact I think there is a good possibility they grew up together. We will deal with it in depth later, but I think that Zacharias, John's father died within a few years of his son's birth. If he did die, as I believe, then Elizabeth would have been left a widow with an infant son. She would need help and would most likely turn to her relatives for that help. Her father or mother's sister or bother's daughter (Mary) might be that relative. So, it is possible that Jesus and his cousin John spent their youth and early manhood together until John went off into the desert and began to preach the coming of the Christ.

Yet, in spite of the above, it would seem from this questioning by John that he was at least not sure at this point. I have little doubt that Christ's enemies where spreading false lies about Him and that some of these came to John's ear. Doubts can rear their ugly head in all of us. I read where Mother Teresa had doubts. But like Mother Teresa and John we should not let those doubts stop us from doing what is right. There is an old saying to the effect that virtue is its own reward. Doing good is good. If doubts assail you, don't cease your good works while you wait for them to subside. The good works are in themselves godly and will tend to crowd out the doubts and fears. If we hold to the iron rod through the darkness of doubt we will eventually find our way to the light of faith again.

20 When the men were come unto him, they said, John the Baptist hath sent us unto thee, saying, Art thou he that should come? or look we for another?
21 And in that same hour he cured many of their infirmities and plagues, and of evil spirits; and unto many that were blind he gave sight.
22 Then Jesus answering said unto them, Go your way, and tell John what things ye have seen and heard; how that the blind see, the lame walk, the lepers are cleansed, the deaf hear, the dead are raised, to the poor the gospel is preached.

Apparently, Christ did not give them an immediate reply to their question, instead asking them to stand aside and watch a while, and then go tell John what they saw.

I have to say it again. I know I get to repeating myself, but here it is again. Notice what the savior says to tell John. John wants to know if this is what he has been waiting for. How does Christ reply? Does he tell John's disciples to go and tell him that Christ said, "Last week we had a 140 in Sunday School. The offering plates were full. I preached on the error of transubstantiation and the truth of consubstantiation. This week's sermon is on the virgin birth. Next week I preach on the trinity." No, he makes no mention of catechizing, or indoctrination, no mention of not eating with sinners or Sabbath keeping. Just a list of ways people have been helped. We, too, show the world ours is the true religion by the way we help people. The world is watching us just like those two disciples of John watched Christ, but are they seeing us ministering as Christ was? James says, (James 1:27) "Pure religion and undefiled before God and the Father is this, To visit the fatherless and widows in their affliction..." To be ministering, in other words, to be taking care of others. That is the test I must pass and you have to pass.

23 And blessed is he, whosoever shall not be offended in me.

Who would be offened? Pharisees. They were the doctrinal theologians of their day. But Christ ignored what they thought was important and instead ministered to the people's needs.

24 And when the messengers of John were departed, he began to speak unto the people concerning John, What went ye out into the wilderness for to see? A reed shaken with the wind?
25 But what went ye out for to see? A man clothed in soft raiment? Behold, they which are gorgeously appareled, and live delicately, are in kings' courts.
26 But what went ye out for to see? A prophet? Yea, I say unto you, and much more than a prophet.
27 This is he, of whom it is written, Behold, I send my messenger before thy face, which shall prepare thy way before thee.
28 For I say unto you, Among those that are born of women there

is not a greater prophet than John the Baptist: but he that is least in the kingdom of God is greater than he.

This is a confusing passage. I am not sure what the Savior is saying. Let me offer a possibility. I have heard those that say Christ is speaking of before Himself and after. That those who have the New Testament Gospel have so much more than those that lived under the Old Testament Law, that the least of the latter is greater than the best of former. That may be what He is saying. At any rate I do not believe the Savior is in anyway putting down John. He is holding him up as an example, while saying the future holds real hope and will be so much better.

29 And all the people that heard him, and the publicans, justified God, being baptized with the baptism of John.
30 But the Pharisees and lawyers rejected the counsel of God against themselves, being not baptized of him.
31 And the Lord said, Whereunto then shall I liken the men of this generation? and to what are they like?
32 They are like unto children sitting in the marketplace, and calling one to another, and saying, We have piped unto you, and ye have not danced; we have mourned to you, and ye have not wept.
33 **For John the Baptist came neither eating bread nor drinking wine; and ye say, He hath a devil.**
34 **The Son of man is come eating and drinking; and ye say, Behold a gluttonous man, and a winebibber, a friend of publicans and sinners!**

If someone does not want to convert they can always find a reason. The easiest and best way to justify a decision not to follow Christ is to find fault with those who have already started down that path. Look at "Christians," see their short comings and say they are worse than I or at least no better than I, so why bother. That is one of

Satan's best tools for keeping from following Christ, by pointing out to them the short comings of others.

On another topic this passage brings to mind. Christ is talking about two extremes. John lives in the desert and eats locusts and honey. Christ is found in the cities and keeping company with people some others find disagreeable. I think the church has to steer a course between extremes. If the church is so unlike anything people know or understand it will be avoided as being alien. If however, it is so like everything else people see, offers no choices, then they will take a why bother attitude. There has to be something there worth getting up for on Sunday morning, something different, but not too different.

35 But wisdom is justified of all her children.
**36 And one of the Pharisees desired him that he would eat with him. And he went into the Pharisee's house, and sat down to meat.
37 And, behold, a woman in the city, which was a sinner, when she knew that Jesus sat at meat in the Pharisee's house, brought an alabaster box of ointment,
38 And stood at his feet behind him weeping, and began to wash his feet with tears, and did wipe them with the hairs of her head, and kissed his feet, and anointed them with the ointment.
39 Now when the Pharisee which had bidden him saw it, he spake within himself, saying, This man, if he were a prophet, would have known who and what manner of woman this is that toucheth him: for she is a sinner.**

A couple thoughts here. Why is a "sinner" in the Pharisee's home? Could it be part of a test by the Pharisee? It doesn't read that way. I really do not know what she is doing there. I can only guess she heard of Jesus' presence and snuck in. However she got there, the important thing is that she is sorrowful for her sins and is trying to honor Christ the Lord. This is what the Lord wants of all of us.

Repentance and good works that demonstrates that we are trying to do better.

Might this be Mary Magdalene? The scriptures don't say so, but I like to think it is. The scriptures intimate that Mary came from a dark background. But she saw in Christ her Savior. I like the idea that in this passage we see Mary's repentance and the life changing experience that made her a disciple, and not just any disciple, but the one that Christ first appeared to after His resurrection, not Peter who would lead His church, not John the Beloved, but Mary (his wife???).

As to that wife thing, many reject it out of hand, and won't even consider the idea. I do not know why. There were early Christian sects that thought sex, even between husband and wife, was evil. Some of those attitudes may still linger in Christian thought. However a wife does not make Christ any more or less the Son of God. It seems to me it does make Christ more the Son of Man.

40 And Jesus answering said unto him, Simon, I have somewhat to say unto thee. And he saith, Master, say on.
41 There was a certain creditor which had two debtors: the one owed five hundred pence, and the other fifty.
42 And when they had nothing to pay, he frankly forgave them both. Tell me therefore, which of them will love him most?
43 Simon answered and said, I suppose that he, to whom he forgave most. And he said unto him, Thou hast rightly judged.
44 And he turned to the woman, and said unto Simon, Seest thou this woman? I entered into thine house, thou gavest me no water for my feet: but she hath washed my feet with tears, and wiped them with the hairs of her head.
45 Thou gavest me no kiss: but this woman since the time I came in hath not ceased to kiss my feet.
46 My head with oil thou didst not anoint: but this woman hath

anointed my feet with ointment.
47 Wherefore I say unto thee, Her sins, which are many, are forgiven; for she loved much: but to whom little is forgiven, the same loveth little.
48 And he said unto her, Thy sins are forgiven.
49 And they that sat at meat with him began to say within themselves, Who is this that forgiveth sins also?
50 And he said to the woman, Thy faith hath saved thee; go in peace.

Such a great story, and so true. The more we are forgiven the more grateful we are or should be. Her sins, which are many, are forgiven: for she loved much: but to whom little is forgiven, the same loveth little. Some great Christians have come from very bad backgrounds. John Newton was a slaver. You can't get much lower than that. He found Christ and wrote Amazing Grace, probably the best loved hymn of Christianity. He could truly say, "Amazing Grace, how sweet the sound that saved a wretch like me."

However, my personal favorite hymn isn't Amazing Grace, it is Charles Wesley's And Can It Be. My favorite verse goes:

Long my imprisioned spirit lay,
Fast bound in sin and nature's night;
Thine eye diffused a quickening ray –
I woke, the dungeon flamed with light;
My chains fell off, my heart was free,
I rose, went forth, and followed thee.
Amazing love, how can it be,
That thou my God shouldst die for me.

Can't you just hear Mary, or whomever the woman was who ministered to Christ, saying, or better yet singing those very words? I can.

Chapter 8

1 And it came to pass afterward, that he went throughout every city and village, preaching and shewing the glad tidings of the kingdom of God: and the twelve were with him,

2 **And certain women, which had been healed of evil spirits and infirmities, Mary called Magdalene, out of whom went seven devils,**

You have probably noticed I tend to get on an issue and ride it. So while I am still in the saddle, let me say that I wrote the previous comments without reading ahead to see the verses in context. Probably a mistake on my part. However, now I do read what comes next and viola I find this passage that just seems to follow on so well with the idea that the woman who ministered to Christ was Mary Magdalene. Christ cast seven demons out of her. As best I can tell, demons usually effect the mind, causing mental illness. Mary had not one, but seven demons. How tortured and individual she must have been. Then Christ finds her in her misery and frees her from their influence. How hopeless she must have felt before that fateful meeting. How wonderful she must have felt afterwards. Wouldn't you want to worship the Man who could do that for you? Wouldn't you buy some ointment and anoint His feet. Of course, you would.

3 And Joanna the wife of Chuza Herod's steward, and Susanna, and

many others, which ministered unto him of their substance.

4 And when much people were gathered together, and were come to him out of every city, he spake by a parable:

5 **A sower went out to sow his seed: and as he sowed, some fell by the way side; and it was trodden down, and the fowls of the air devoured it.**

6 **And some fell upon a rock; and as soon as it was sprung up, it withered away, because it lacked moisture.**

7 **And some fell among thorns; and the thorns sprang up with it, and choked it.**

8 **And other fell on good ground, and sprang up, and bare fruit an hundredfold. And when he had said these things, he cried, He that hath ears to hear, let him hear.**

9 **And his disciples asked him, saying, What might this parable be?**

10 **And he said, Unto you it is given to know the mysteries of the kingdom of God: but to others in parables; that seeing they might not see, and hearing they might not understand.**

11 **Now the parable is this: The seed is the word of God.**

12 **Those by the way side are they that hear; then cometh the devil, and taketh away the word out of their hearts, lest they should believe and be saved.**

13 **They on the rock are they, which, when they hear, receive the word with joy; and these have no root, which for a while believe, and in time of temptation fall away.**

14 **And that which fell among thorns are they, which, when they have heard, go forth, and are choked with cares and riches and pleasures of this life, and bring no fruit to perfection.**

15 **But that on the good ground are they, which in an honest and good heart, having heard the word, keep it, and bring forth fruit with patience.**

I would guess that the above is one of the top ten passages used

as the textual basis for sermons to be built upon. Preachers love it.
They thunder forth their message to the congregation of seeds in their
pews, attempting to frighten them. "Make sure you are on deep, weed
free soil," they tell their listeners.

Could it be, however, that they are missing the whole point of
the parable. When you think about it everyone knows it is not possible
for a seed to control its flight and where it lands as it is being sown.
Nor can a plant pick itself up by the roots and move itself to fertile soil.
There is only one way for the seeds that fell on shallow soil or among
weeds to survive. That is for the farmers themselves to intervene.
He/She can add more moisture holding soil to the areas among the
rocks. He/She can pull the thorns around the seeds that fell into a weed
patch. He/she can transplant the young plants from the shallow soil or
weedy soil to a more fertile location. One of these three are needed or
the seeds that landed in the wrong area are doomed through no fault of
their own.

Bishops, parents, teachers, pastors, or whoever is spreading the
seed of the gospel, your job is not done went the sowing is over.
Wringing your hands and going, "Oh, alas, alas," over the seed in dry,
rocky, or weedy ground is not the answer. Those wayward seeds are
like the lost sheep. They need your help.

It should also be noted that there is another way to deal with the
situation such as Christ describes. Be proactive. Before sowing the
seeds in the first place, the rocks can be collected and piled elsewhere.
The weeds can be harrowed and dug out. In short, the ground can be
better prepared than the field of the farmer Christ describes. All of the
above should be employed to save the precious seed from being wasted.

I love the beautiful pictures you see of small family farms in
Ireland and elsewhere. Rich black earth is exposed or green plants are

growing in a checkerboard field with small areas for growing separated by fences of rocks. It did not get that way very quickly. These rocks have been collected from the growing areas over the years, or more probably over many many generations. When a plow turns up a rock the farmer doesn't just go around, he picks it up and carries it to the fence and adds it to what is already there. Initially the rocks were everywhere making growing crops difficult. But effort was put in to remove them from the growing area. They are heavy and hauling them long distances difficult so the fences of collected rocks criss cross the fields. As time goes on wind and rain carry away soil and new rocks that were too deep to matter are now turned over by the plow and removed to be come part of the fence. Thus the process goes on.

The plowing and the removal of the rocks makes the soil in the small plantings between the fences excellent growing areas. What was originally probably not very farmer friendly becomes a wonderful area to grow things. Isn't preparing an area to grow crops a better idea than scattering the seed first and then lamenting that some seed is going to waste, or trying to rescue the seed after planting? The seed is the gospel and the gospel is precious and not to be wasted.

16 No man, when he hath lighted a candle, covereth it with a vessel, or putteth it under a bed; but setteth it on a candlestick, that they which enter in may see the light.

We live in an age when light is just taken for granted. Christ lived in an age lit only by fire. When the sun went down it got dark and stayed that way till dawn. It must have been a strange and frightening way to live. So if you have a candle or oil lamp you share it. Nobody enjoys the dark. All are attracted to the light.

We have invented the electric light for our physical lives, however the spiritual portion of our existence is still in the dark ages. If

17 For nothing is secret, that shall not be made manifest; neither any thing hid, that shall not be known and come abroad.

18 Take heed therefore how ye hear: for whosoever hath, to him shall be given; and whosoever hath not, from him shall be taken even that which he seemeth to have.

19 Then came to him his mother and his brethren, and could not come at him for the press.

20 And it was told him by certain which said, Thy mother and thy brethren stand without, desiring to see thee.

21 And he answered and said unto them, My mother and my **brethren** are these which hear the word of God, and do it.

22 Now it came to pass on a certain day, that he went into a ship with his disciples: and he said unto them, Let us go over unto the other side of the lake. And they launched forth.

23 But as they sailed he fell asleep: and there came down a storm of wind on the lake; and they were filled with water, and were in jeopardy.

24 And they came to him, and awoke him, saying, Master, master, we perish. Then he arose, and rebuked the wind and the raging of the water: and they ceased, and there was a calm.

25 And he said unto them, Where is your faith? And they being afraid wondered, saying one to another, What manner of man is this! for he commandeth even the winds and water, and they obey him.

26 **And they arrived at the country of the Gadarenes, which is over against Galilee.**

27 **And when he went forth to land, there met him out of the city a certain man, which had devils long time, and ware no clothes, neither abode in any house, but in the tombs.**

28 **When he saw Jesus, he cried out, and fell down before him, and with a loud voice said, What have I to do with thee, Jesus, thou Son of God most high? I beseech thee, torment me not.**

29 (For he had commanded the unclean spirit to come out of the
man. For oftentimes it had caught him: and he was kept bound
with chains and in fetters; and he brake the bands, and was driven
of the devil into the wilderness.)
30 And Jesus asked him, saying, What is thy name? And he said,
Legion: because many devils were entered into him.
31 And they besought him that he would not command them to go
out into the deep.
32 And there was there an herd of many swine feeding on the
mountain: and they besought him that he would suffer them to
enter into them. And he suffered them.
33 Then went the devils out of the man, and entered into the
swine: and the herd ran violently down a steep place into the lake,
and were choked.

*Time and again in the Gospels we find demons that recognize
Christ for who he is while even his disciples don't seem to realize just
who they are following. Why are these demons smarter than men? I
don't know. They are not all wise all knowing creatures, take this
bunch. They know that Christ is about to cast them out and they do not
want to be sent down into the sea. "Send us into the swine instead,"
they plead. Their wish is granted but then the swine run down into the
sea and drown. So the result is the same except there is now a herd of
dead pigs too. So then, demons aren't as clever as they think they are,
but they seem to have better spiritual eyes than men. This is something I
do not understand.*

34 When they that fed them saw what was done, they fled, and
went and told it in the city and in the country.
35 Then they went out to see what was done; and came to Jesus,
and found the man, out of whom the devils were departed, sitting at
the feet of Jesus, clothed, and in his right mind: and they were
afraid.

36 They also which saw it told them by what means he that was possessed of the devils was healed.

37 Then the whole multitude of the country of the Gadarenes round about besought him to depart from them; for they were taken with great fear: and he went up into the ship, and returned back again.

The "country of the Gadarenes" is not a Jewish area. It is my understanding that they were a Gentile people that lived around the shore of The Sea of Galilee from Capernaum which was a Jewish area. Why Jesus would want to go there I do not know. Storm damage to the boat? A need to get away from the crowds? Knowing there is a man there that needed His help? Some other reason? At any rate Christ and his disciples arrive there and find the demon possessed man living among the tombs. (Tombs in Christ's day were different than what they are like today. Usually in Christ's time they were a hollowed out tunnel in the rock with platforms carved in the sides to lay bodies out. A family would have one for their dead. However, space was limited and over time many bodies would need a place to be placed. So, when someone died they would not be buried in the ground, but placed on one of the platforms in the tomb and left to decay. In about a year there would be just bones left which were then collected and placed in a stone bone box called a ossuary. The platform was then free to be used again for the next family member to die.) I think the clear implication of the text is that he didn't live in a graveyard as we think of one today, he sheltered inside the tombs. This gives us some idea of depths the demons had taken him to. What he called home was in fact a tunnel full of rotting corpses. Christ saves him from this condition, casting the demons out and sending them into the swine.

So how do the people of the area react. The swineherds have a reason to be upset. They have lost their way of living. But isn't saving a man worth the lives of the swine. I would say so. Not to the Gadarenes,

We talk of the milk of human kindness but we rarely see it. Instead of celebrating the man's recovery, the people ask Christ to leave the area. It is interesting that they "besought" Him to leave. They asked. They did not try to drive him away, just said "please go."

As I am writing this the world is undergoing a pandemic. People have been told to go home and stay there with no physical contact with neighbors, friends, extended family, and not to go to your job. It has been terrible for our nations economy. Now that the worst seems to be behind us people want the restrictions lifted, even if it means more will catch the disease. Money is more important than those who will die. Sad.

38 Now the man out of whom the devils were departed besought him that he might be with him: but Jesus sent him away, saying, 39 Return to thine own house, and shew how great things God hath done unto thee. And he went his way, and published throughout the whole city how great things Jesus had done unto him.

Two things of note here: 1) Jesus sends a Gentile to tell Gentiles about what the Jewish God had done for him. This man may be the first of a line that would stretch to Luke, who's gospel we are reading, and on beyond to today. 2) I have to wonder if the above (telling the man to tell his neighbors what God has done for him) would have taken place if the Gadarenes had not been respectful in their dealing with Christ. There is a lot of talk in the Old Testament about "Fearing" God. I think a better translation would be to "Respect" God. The God I worship does not want me to go around shaking in my boots as I worship Him. But I think he wants a servant that knows there is a difference between Him and I and is mindful of that difference.

40 And it came to pass, that, when Jesus was returned, the people gladly received him: for they were all waiting for him.

41 And, behold, there came a man named Jairus, and he was a ruler of the synagogue: and he fell down at Jesus' feet, and besought him that he would come into his house:

42 For he had one only daughter, about twelve years of age, and she lay a dying. But as he went the people thronged him.

43 And a woman having an issue of blood twelve years, which had spent all her living upon physicians, neither could be healed of any,

44 Came behind him, and touched the border of his garment: and immediately her issue of blood stanched.

45 And Jesus said, Who touched me? When all denied, Peter and they that were with him said, Master, the multitude throng thee and press thee, and sayest thou, Who touched me?

46 And Jesus said, Somebody hath touched me: for I perceive that virtue is gone out of me.

47 And when the woman saw that she was not hid, she came trembling, and falling down before him, she declared unto him before all the people for what cause she had touched him and how she was healed immediately.

48 And he said unto her, Daughter, be of good comfort: thy faith hath made thee whole; go in peace.

49 While he yet spake, there cometh one from the ruler of the synagogue's house, saying to him, Thy daughter is dead; trouble not the Master.

50 But when Jesus heard it, he answered him, saying, Fear not: believe only, and she shall be made whole.

51 And when he came into the house, he suffered no man to go in, save Peter, and James, and John, and the father and the mother of the maiden.

52 And all wept, and bewailed her: but he said, Weep not; she is

not dead, but sleepeth.

53 **And they laughed him to scorn, knowing that she was dead.**

54 **And he put them all out, and took her by the hand, and called, saying, Maid, arise.**

55 **And her spirit came again, and she arose straightway: and he commanded to give her meat.**

56 **And her parents were astonished: but he charged them that they should tell no man what was done.**

We find two stories here and I would like to write of both of them.

Let's take Jairus first. This is not a man we would expect to have come to Christ for help. By this time in His ministry Christ's emphasis on living a good life, not on following a strict set of rules/doctrines has made enemies of those who would keep the throngs in line by forcing strict compliance with those rules. They thought Jesus was a Sabbath breaker. He took his message to people looked down on by the rule keepers. He did other things they took issue with too. (We see all this build to a head till they finally demand the Romans crucify Christ).

So, then, a day comes when one of the leaders of the religious class has a daughter who is mortally ill. He no doubt prays but the girl does not get better, she gets worse. He may promise to go to Jerusalem and offer sacrifices. I would. How many times a day does Heavenly Father hear one of His children offering some sort of deal. If only God will this, the petitioner will do that. The offers are sincere, but the deals seldom made. I am sure Jairus calls in doctors too, but they are no help.

He's heard that this sinner Jesus can heal the sick. But that is just it, the man is a sinner. How can he work miracles? Still people say he does. But his daughter, whom he no doubt loves, is dying and in desperation he will do anything, even go to a sinner for help. In a similar situation so would I and most of you reading this. Principles are okay, but where our loved ones health and safety are concerned many will cut corners. I think something like I outlined above transpired before Jairus finally comes in desperation and falls to his knees in front of Jesus.

We do not read where Jesus admonishes Jairus in any way. This is Christ's chance to score points. Does he? No, he simply lets the man lead him to his house. While they are on the way to the home word comes that the girl has died. Jesus says don't worry, believe and she will be made whole. When they get to the house, Christ lets the father and mother and three disciples join him in the home. There the body lays. Jesus tells them she only sleeps but they laugh at Him because she's obviously dead. They can see that for themselves. (I think that "they" that laugh are the father and mother, not the disciples who have seen Jesus restore the dead to life, and so wouldn't laugh, but instead anticipate another miracle.) A desperate man has taken desperate means to try to save a beloved daughter and failed. He laughs at Jesus, but even more so, he is laughing at himself. "I went to a sinner and this is what I get." Luke does not tell us that is what is going through Jairus mind, and probably that of his wife too, but I know human nature well enough to read between the lines here.

Jesus tells them all to get out then reaches out to the girl and restores her life. He takes the girl to her family and says she needs something to eat. No "I told you so." He does not rub it in. If there was ever a man who disserved to loose his daughter this is the one. He is part of the cabal that will take Christ's life. But there is no visiting the sins of the father on the child.

Jesus shows himself as completely magnanimous throughout this incident.

Now, back to the story. In the middle of the happenings around Jairus and his daughter something else is going on. There is a woman with an "issue of blood." I do not know for sure what this means, but I think she probably either had a wound that would not heal, or suffered constant menstrual bleeding. At any rate I think its safe to say she was constantly bleeding for some reason. Someplace on her body she is slowly bleedubg because she'd had the condidtion for twelve years and yet has not bled to death.

Now Jewish people believed that if you were bleeding you were "unclean" and had to separate yourself from society. Women did so regularly when they had their cycle. If I remember correctly a menstruating woman had to lock herself away for about a week. If a woman delivered a baby, that being a much more bloody process, she would isolate herself for about a month. If for some reason they had to go out into places where other people were during their time of isolation, they were supposed to cry, "Unclean" as a warning to others to stay away from them. If you touched or were touched by an "unclean" person you became unclean yourself and had to go through a ritual cleansing to remove the taint. (It is interesting to note that those with leprosy also had to cry "unclean" so people would know to stay away from them.)

There is nothing in Luke's gospel to indicate that this woman was crying "Unclean" to warn others off. You have to ask yourself why? I believe the answer is she wanted to get close to Jesus because she believed that where all her doctors had failed, that He could heal her. But if she followed the rules, and cried out, everyone would avoid her, even Jesus. Or at least I think that is what she thought.

So she works her way through the crowd around Jesus, I believe she came up behind Him and reached out to touch his robe.

Immediately she is cured. How she knows this is a mystery. Suffice to say she knows. Her faith has been the conduit for her healing.

But something strange goes on here. Jesus asks "Who touched me?" Why would an all knowing being ask any question? Since I think Jesus is God and is all knowing, we have to assume the question is rhetorical. He knows but has a point to make and gets the conversation started in this way, asking a question he already knows the answer to. Of course the disciples think in small terms. They always do. They tell him, hey look at this crowd surrounding you, and you want to know who touched. The implication they are making is it could be anybody.

*Now two interesting things happen. First He says "**for I perceive that virtue is gone out of me.**" That is a confusing statement. What does he mean by "virtue?" I believe in the old English virtue and power are two words that could be used interchangeably. That is no longer true, the meaning of virtue has changed. So if the King James Bible translators could have looked down the corridors of time and seen how the word virtue would change in meaning they might have used the word power instead. I like to think so. Christ's statement would then make more sense too modern readers.*

Secondly, the woman comes and falls at Christ's feet and confesses, not just that it was her that touched Him, but why she did. In doing so she is saying that she was not following the rules and warning people of her condition. In desperation she ignored the rules as she sought help. She is the second person healed in this portion of scripture and she is the second to violate their societal rules or personal beliefs as they came to the savior for help and neither is turned away without the asked for help.

How many churches today, or individuals offer help but it comes with strings? Christ did not require obedience to a dogma or rules to receive His help. It came freely. There is a lesson her for us

Chapter 9

1 Then he called his twelve disciples together, and gave them power and authority over all devils, and to cure diseases.
2 And he sent them to preach the kingdom of God, and to heal the sick.
3 And he said unto them, Take nothing for your journey, neither staves, nor scrip, neither bread, neither money; neither have two coats apiece.
4 And whatsoever house ye enter into, there abide, and thence depart.

When my church first sent out missionaries they went much the same as Christ's disciples. These men went out to preach the gospel and demonstrated the power of the Spirit by healing the sick and casting out demons. And they went in faith, taking nothing to support themselves along the way, relying on the spirit to move people to feed and shelter them as they went.

Times have changed and the mission field has changed a great deal since that time almost 200 years ago. Then "hospitality" was common on the frontier. People would open their homes to strangers, especially ones with a tale to tell. Religion was important to people but they weren't blindly accepting what they had. They detected the shallowness of most churches and congregations. They knew there must be something more. So when a couple missionaries came to their door and told them of a "Restored Gospel" it would not be uncommon for those missionaries to be invited in for supper and the night so the people could hear more of what they had to say (Remember this was a day of no TV or Radio. Most homes had just one book, the Bible. Folks were starved for news and information.) After the meal they would all gather before the fire and hear the story of the restoration of the church to that of the New Testament times. They would also hear of the Book of Mormon and the Prophet Joseph Smith. Some would believe and some wouldn't. If there was enough interest in the area the missionaries would stay, moving from house to house sharing the gospel. Most back woods areas couldn't support a full time pastor and had to rely on circuit riding preachers that only showed up every month or two to preach. Most Sundays these folks were on their own and so they could and did invite the missionaries to hold the Sunday Service for them. The missionaries would baptize all that came to the gospel. The circuit riding preacher would eventually show up and be appalled to find his congregation, or at least a sizable portion thereof were now Mormon.

Today an invitation to stay the night would be very unusual. Only someone actively seeking truth would be even likely to invite the missionaries in. An opportunity to conduct the services for a church on Sunday would be almost unheard of. So today's missionaries are supported by their families and others in the church. They do not live high on the hog, but neither do they rely people's generosity to live. They are provided enough to live modestly and are thus freed to spend their time spreading the gospel, and seeking out those that are searching for the truth.

5 And whosoever will not receive you, when ye go out of that city, shake off the very dust from your feet for a testimony against them.
6 And they departed, and went through the towns, preaching the gospel, and healing everywhere.
7 **Now Herod the tetrarch heard of all that was done by him: and he was perplexed, because that it was said of some, that John was risen from the dead;**

8 **And of some, that Elias had appeared; and of others, that one of the old prophets was risen again.**

9 **And Herod said, John have I beheaded: but who is this, of whom I hear such things? And he desired to see him.**

I do not think that I have to say much about Herod (by the way, there were a lot of them by that name, and none of them any good). This one was responsible for the killing of John the Baptist, a tale Luke left out of his gospel but you can find in the 14th chapter of Matthew's gospel. What I find interesting in this passage is what Herod is told when he asks who this Christ is. John the Baptist come back to life he is told, or Elias (read Elijah) come back from the dead, or some other prophet arisen from the grave and performing miracles. Nothing about this being the Son of God come to dwell among us and show us how to live.

How like humans. We have little use for our contemporaries. Most of the Church today thinks God quit speaking to man when Saint John finished writing the Book or Revelation. Admittedly such a belief can save a lot of problems. If someone comes along and claims to speak for Heavenly Father you can reject them and take no notice of what they say out of hand, claiming God shut up some two thousand years ago. It offers a convenient and useful escape. You do not have to judge what this person says, just point out that there are no modern revelations, therefore they are deluded, and can be dismissed without a second thought.

The problem is that this "no new revelations" and thus a silent God are not Biblical concepts. The scriptures do not teach that idea. It is merely a manmade construct designed to cut off debate. To say God still speaks to His children is to allow wild cards into the deck. No idea can be considered safe or set in concrete if we allow for the new revelations. We like things the way they are (religiously speaking) and can't have Heavenly Father coming down and stirring the pot with new ideas.

Thankfully a few of us believe otherwise. We think that Heavenly Father does have prophets, seers, and revelators for modern man just as there were for those in Biblical times. And why shouldn't there be? Have we reached some higher plane of religious existence where we no longer need God to speak to us. Are we at the point where all we need to do is say we are sorry for our sins, and then follow the rules and learn the dogma. As for God, in providing for our salvation, He has done His part, and now is relegated to just getting our mansions ready for us?

I think not. God is interested in us as His children both individually and as a group. He will speak us about our personal lives and to us as His church about our collective lives. God still speaks.

10 And the apostles, when they were returned, told him all that they had done. And he took them, and went aside privately into a desert place belonging to the city called Bethsaida.

11 And the people, when they knew it, followed him: and he received them, and spake unto them of the kingdom of God, and healed them that had need of healing.

12 And when the day began to wear away, then came the twelve, and said unto him, Send the multitude away, that they may go into the towns and country round about, and lodge, and get victuals: for we are here in a desert place.

13 But he said unto them, Give ye them to eat. And they said, We have no more but five loaves and two fishes; except we should go and buy meat for all this people.

14 For they were about five thousand men. And he said to his disciples, Make them sit down by fifties in a company.

15 And they did so, and made them all sit down.

16 Then he took the five loaves and the two fishes, and looking up to heaven, he blessed them, and brake, and gave to the disciples to set before the multitude.

17 And they did eat, and were all filled: and there was taken up of fragments that remained to them twelve baskets.

18 And it came to pass, as he was alone praying, his disciples were with him: and he asked them, saying, Whom say the people that I am?

19 They answering said, John the Baptist; but some say, Elias; and others say, that one of the old prophets is risen again.

20 He said unto them, But whom say ye that I am? Peter answering said, The Christ of God.

See the last passage where we discussed people's inability to see Christ for who He was. Thankfully Peter understood the truth. When he said Jesus was "The Christ of God," he is saying to Him you are the Messiah. You are the one sent from God the Father. You are the one promised to our fathers that would come and set up the Kingdom of God on earth.

*Implied in Peter's remark is that Christ has not come to just assume the existing throne of the government or the leadership of the existing religious order. He is come to make some changes in how things are done. In government a king or emperor is not the ideal. We know from modern revelations that God moved in the formation of the United States to prepare a fertile ground for His restoration of the Gospel and the True Church. We know he was instrumental in the formation of this country and no doubt had a part in writing the Declaration of Independence. I think I detect His inspiration in the most noble words found anywhere in the world outside of the Scriptures. Those words being the foundation our nation is built on: **We hold these truths to be self-evident, that all men are created equal, that they are*** *endowed by their Creator with certain unalienable Rights, that among these are Life, Liberty and the pursuit of Happiness.--That to secure these rights, Governments are instituted among Men, deriving their just powers from the consent of the governed.*

Nor did Jesus come to just assume the role of Jewish High Priest (He was of the wrong Tribe of Israel for that anyway, the priesthood in those days being held by the Levites, while Christ was born into the Tribe of Judah). As we have already discussed numerous times in this treatise, Jesus had a different message, one of lifestyle and not of doctrine.

Christianity has led to new and better forms of government and religion.

21 And he straitly charged them, and commanded them to tell no man that thing;

22 Saying, The Son of man must suffer many things, and be rejected of the elders and chief priests and scribes, and be slain, and be raised the third day.

23 **And he said to them all, If any man will come after me, let him deny himself, and take up his cross daily, and follow me.**

24 **For whosoever will save his life shall lose it: but whosoever will lose his life for my sake, the same shall save it.**

25 **For what is a man advantaged, if he gain the whole world, and lose himself, or be cast away?**

26 **For whosoever shall be ashamed of me and of my words, of him shall the Son of man be ashamed, when he shall come in his own glory, and in his Father's, and of the holy angels.**

The Gospel that Jesus taught was not without its obligations. He did not demand doctrinal purity, but he did ask a lot of his followers. He asked them to follow a lifestyle very different from their fellow beings. One of the most important traits of the "Christian" lifestyle is self-denial. I believe that this is manifest in helping others. Elsewhere in the scriptures a rich young man comes to Him and says he wants to become a disciple. Jesus tells him to sell all he has, give the proceeds to the poor, and then come follow Him. Another time he says it is easier for a camel to go through the eye of a needle than it is for a rich man to make it into the Kingdom of God. If a literal sowing needle is what Jesus was speaking of then it would be absolutely impossible for a rich person to make it to heaven. However "the eye of the needle" is also a name often given to a small gate in a city's walls. At night the main gate was closed so an enemy could not break-in and overwhelm a city while they slept. But people realized that visitors might show up at any hour. This small gate was used by the night guards to let visitors in after the main gate was closed. It was deliberately low and small so somebody would have to crouch over to use it. It could be easily defended. It was nearly, but not completely impossible, for someone showing up with a camel to get the beast down on its knees and through the Eye of the Needle gate. It could be done, but it was a lot of work. This is what Christ is saying.

If we look back at history, we find many examples of how not to follow Christ in this matter. Take the Puritans as an example. They, contrary to the scriptures we just discussed, believed "it was Godly to be rich." Their hope of attaining heaven was based on their doctrinal purity. They believed the Church of England, and the Roman Catholic Church were both evils, and they alone had a proper grasp of doctrinal issues. Surely God would honor them for taking this virtuous stand against error.

I have spent a great deal of time searching my genealogy. I am very interested to learn about my roots and where I came from. In my research I came on an interesting and, I think, humorous story of my family when they lived in Puritan times. My ancestors arrived in New

England in about 1638 and settled in (actually helped found) Milford, Connecticut. As I said above, Puritans thought it godly to be rich. However, those rich ones were jealous for their status in their communities. That being the case they made it a law that you had to be personally worth at least 200 Pounds (a good deal on money in those days) to be entitled to wear silk clothes. It seems my 9th great aunt was admonished in court for wearing silk contrary to the law. She was tried for her crime of "wearing it in a flaunting manner and excess of apparel to the offence of sober people."

How different from Christ's denying of self, and taking up a cross and following him, is the Puritan society mentioned above. Both sides were in the wrong and displayed UnChrist like behavior. My nine times great aunt for spending money on very fancy clothes and her society for placing such emphasis on wealth, that it brought with itself certain prerogatives denied to others.

Even today, I do not think we are so far from those old Puritans. How many of us do not envy the rich?

I like to think this devotional commentary is not dated. I hesitate to put in references that in a few months or years will mean nothing. However, I have to, at this juncture point out, that at this time one of our political parties is seriously considering nominating a billionaire as their candidate for President of the United States. His main claim to leadership is his accumulation of wealth and the skills that allowed him to do so. His money and his ability to make money may result in him living in the White House. We call ourselves a "Christian" nation, but I have to wonder how this modern definition of Christianity comports with the actual teachings of Christ.

27 But I tell you of a truth, there be some standing here, which shall not taste of death, till they see the kingdom of God.

Some people believe this it a reference to Saint John and that he is somehow still living after these two thousand years. I doubt that he still lives, and if he did still live, then why he would be in hiding and not out fulfilling the marching orders Christ gave him and the rest of his disciples: Go ye therefore into all the world and preach the gospel.

I think it makes more sense to take John's Book of Revelation as the fulfillment of the prophecy Christ made. John clearly was shown the Kingdom as part of the writing of the book.

28 And it came to pass about an eight days after these sayings, he took Peter and John and James, and went up into a mountain to pray.

29 And as he prayed, the fashion of his countenance was altered, and his raiment was white and glistering.

30 And, behold, there talked with him two men, which were Moses and Elias:

31 Who appeared in glory, and spake of his decease which he should accomplish at Jerusalem.

32 But Peter and they that were with him were heavy with sleep: and when they were awake, they saw his glory, and the two men that stood with him.

33 And it came to pass, as they departed from him, Peter said unto Jesus, Master, it is good for us to be here: and let us make three tabernacles; one for thee, and one for Moses, and one for Elias: not knowing what he said.

34 While he thus spake, there came a cloud, and overshadowed them: and they feared as they entered into the cloud.

35 And there came a voice out of the cloud, saying, **This is my beloved Son: hear him.**

There are so many voices telling us to listen, and obey,

36 And when the voice was past, Jesus was found alone. And they
kept it close, and told no man in those days any of those things which
they had seen.

37 And it came to pass, that on the next day, when they were come
down from the hill, much people met him.

38 And, behold, a man of the company cried out, saying, Master, I
beseech thee, look upon my son: for he is mine only child.

39 And, lo, a spirit taketh him, and he suddenly crieth out; and it
teareth him that he foameth again, and bruising him hardly departeth
from him.

40 **And I besought thy disciples to cast him out; and they could
not.**

41 **And Jesus answering said, O faithless and perverse generation,
how long shall I be with you, and suffer you? Bring thy son hither.**

*I often find myself wondering at the disciples. They seem so
weak and vacillating and not very bright. I then speculate as to whether
I could have done better. I look at the twelve and say to myself that I
could improve on them. But maybe that is just the benefit of hindsight.
Drop me unprepared into the middle of Christ's earthly ministry and I
might fail too. Then too, they have yet to receive the gift of the Holy
Spirit, and that could be a real game changer. After Pentecost they
stormed out of Jerusalem and spread out across the world and changed
it forever. This same bunch that seemed to stumble at every opportunity
suddenly are changed into earth shaking individuals, and the only thing
that I can see that is different is the gift of the Holy Ghost.*

42 And as he was yet a coming, the devil threw him down, and tare him. And Jesus rebuked the unclean spirit, and healed the child, and delivered him again to his father.

43 And they were all amazed at the mighty power of God. But while they wondered every one at all things which Jesus did, he said unto his disciples,

44 Let these sayings sink down into your ears: for the Son of man shall be delivered into the hands of men.

45 But they understood not this saying, and it was hid from them, that they perceived it not: and they feared to ask him of that saying.

46 Then there arose a reasoning among them, which of them should be greatest.

47 And Jesus, perceiving the thought of their heart, took a child, and set him by him,

48 **And said unto them, Whosoever shall receive this child in my name receiveth me: and whosoever shall receive me receiveth him that sent me: for he that is least among you all, the same shall be great.**

In another of the gospels, this scene is given in different detail. In it Christ tells the disciples that if they want to get into the Kingdom of Heaven, that they have become as the child he set in their midst. The clear implication being that they have to quit worrying about being the greatest disciple (notice they did not wonder who among themselves was the most righteous, or spiritual). Instead Christ tells them if they want to even get into Heaven they need to become childlike followers.

49 **And John answered and said, Master, we saw one casting out devils in thy name; and we forbad him, because he followeth not with us.**

50 **And Jesus said unto him, Forbid him not: for he that is not**

against us is for us.

If he is not one of us there must be something wrong with him and we should rebuke him. That I think would sum up John's views. Christ does not share that opinion. I am reminded of a story I heard about a Christian who dies and goes to the pearly gates. Peter invites him in and guides the man to his heavenly mansion. As they are walking along the golden streets Peter is pointing out the sights. He points and says, "Over hear is where the Baptists are." A little later he shows him where the Catholics are at. Soon they come to an area that has a high wall completely surrounding it. The man asks Peter about the walled off area. Peter shushes him and then whispers, "Quiet. You mustn't make any noise. That's where a certain sect are and they don't think anyone else is here."

Christians are a clannish bunch and each clan (read denomination) think they have a corner on truth. Here we see a man going about doing good even though he is not a member of the official group following Christ. I feel sure there is a good, better, best thing going on here. Christ and his disciples are the best group to be a member of ("The One True Church"), but the others must work too. Steak is better than hot dogs but both will fill you.

51 And it came to pass, when the time was come that he should be received up, he steadfastly set his face to go to Jerusalem,

52 **And sent messengers before his face: and they went, and entered into a village of the Samaritans, to make ready for him.**

53 **And they did not receive him, because his face was as though he would go to Jerusalem.**

54 **And when his disciples James and John saw this, they said, Lord, wilt thou that we command fire to come down from heaven, and consume them, even as Elias did?**

55 **But he turned, and rebuked them, and said, Ye know not what**

manner of spirit ye are of.

56 For the Son of man is not come to destroy men's lives, but to save them. And they went to another village.

This is a passage I have to guess about the context of. The best explanation I can come up with is that this village or maybe its elder wanted Christ to stay awhile but He said, "No, I must keep moving, I have an appointment in Jerusalem." Told this, the villagers refused to open their village to him at all.

Assuming the above is correct I have to say that even though these Samaritans lacked the minimum of hospitality, their lack thereof did not justify the reaction of James and John. I am surprised by what a blood thirsty bunch they are. I must not try to judge them by my societal values. They see things differently. To most Jews of that day Samaritans were trash, mongrels, half Jewish and half Gentile and to be avoided. But that does not justify calling down fire from heaven to consume them. That Christ would spend time in their village was an honor, and yet these ingrates want him to stay awhile or not at all. So let's call down fire on them for their bad manners. Christ, at least, is clearly more enlightened than his followers, for instead of condemning the Samaritans for their lack of hospitality, He condemns instead his own disciples for their cruel attitude.

Thankfully, times have changed and Western Civilization has come to put a premium on life that other ages did not share. Jesus seems closer to my value system than that of His disciples. I chalk our modern standards up to the influence of Christianity. Yet there are lots of places in the world today where life is still cheap, and most of them are areas where Christ's church has not exerted much influence.

57 And it came to pass, that, as they went in the way, a certain man said unto him, Lord, I will follow thee whithersoever thou goest.

58 And Jesus said unto him, Foxes have holes, and birds of the air have nests; but the Son of man hath not where to lay his head.

59 And he said unto another, Follow me. But he said, Lord, suffer me first to go and bury my father.

60 Jesus said unto him, Let the dead bury their dead: but go thou and preach the kingdom of God.

61 And another also said, Lord, I will follow thee; but let me first go bid them farewell, which are at home at my house.

62 And Jesus said unto him, No man, having put his hand to the plough, and looking back, is fit for the kingdom of God.

Three people, three men desirous of being a part of Jesus work, three ready to leave their old lives and follow Jesus even though he has no place to call home. Each, however, has something to take care of first. One thing that Christ demands is absolute devotion.

Chapter 10

1 After these things the Lord appointed other seventy also, and sent them two and two before his face into every city and place, whither he himself would come.

2 Therefore said he unto them, The harvest truly is great, but the labourers are few: pray ye therefore the Lord of the harvest, that he would send forth labourers into his harvest.

3 Go your ways: behold, I send you forth as lambs among wolves.

4 **Carry neither purse, nor scrip, nor shoes**: and salute no man by the way.

When the Church of Jesus Christ of Latter Day Saints was in its infancy, this is how its missionaries went out. I am not sure if that applied to the leaders, but the work a day missionaries went without money and relied on the hospitality of both members and non-members for food and shelter. For the most part this worked because people were more open and unstinting a hundred and fifty years ago. They did not have much but what they did, they shared. Now a days most people look down on anyone without means of taking care of their own needs. For that reason, modern missionaries, both Mormon and Non-Mormon, have enough money to provide for their room and board before they depart. Mormon children begin saving for their missions while very young. They are taught to tithe 10% of any money they receive, and to set apart a portion of the rest in a savings account that they will use to pay for their mission. Any short fall is made up by the church as a whole through our giving.

I am reminded of an experience I had while in college. I joined a group of fellow students that would go into the government housing projects on Saturdays and hold Bible Classes for the children. Then we would go door to door reaching out to people. These projects were full of the poorest people I have been exposed to. (I am sure there are others worse off, but not in my experience). The grounds of the projects had sidewalks and dirt. No grass grew. None. But the ground was latterly covered with broken glass, mainly from various smashed alcoholic beverage bottles. People living there were poor and it bugged them and alcohol was an escape. Drugs were hard to come by in those days in South Carolina, but the booze flowed freely. Especially in the projects.

Anyway, occasionally we would be invited into someone's home to talk. These poor people had little but wanted to share what they had. I can remember drinking from cups that had no handles because they had been broken off. Still they were the best they had and they wanted to share their hospitality. How times have changed.

5 And into whatsoever house ye enter, first say, Peace be to this house.
6 And if the son of peace be there, your peace shall rest upon it: if not, it shall turn to you again.
7 And in the same house remain, eating and drinking such things as they give: for the laborer is worthy of his hire. Go not from house to house.
8 **And into whatsoever city ye enter, and they receive you, eat such things as are set before you:**

I am not sure why the disciples should be told, that when they are in a city or town to eat whatever they are given. I do not think he is telling them to ignore Jewish dietary restrictions. That comes later in a revelation to Peter. He may have reference to food sacrificed to idols. In those days not just the Jews sacrificed animals in their temples. Non Jewish people would bring a cow, or sheep, etc to the local heathen

9 And heal the sick that are therein, and say unto them, The kingdom of God is come nigh unto you.

10 But into whatsoever city ye enter, and they receive you not, go your ways out into the streets of the same, and say,

11 Even the very dust of your city, which cleaveth on us, we do wipe off against you: notwithstanding be ye sure of this, that the kingdom of God is come nigh unto you.

12 But I say unto you, that it shall be more tolerable in that day for Sodom, than for that city.

13 **Woe unto thee, Chorazin! woe unto thee, Bethsaida! for if the mighty works had been done in Tyre and Sidon, which have been done in you, they had a great while ago repented, sitting in sackcloth and ashes.**

14 **But it shall be more tolerable for Tyre and Sidon at the judgment, than for you.**

15 **And thou, Capernaum, which art exalted to heaven, shalt be**

thrust down to hell.

It would be my guess that Christ, knowing what the future held, is saying these cities and towns are going to suffer terrible losses during the Jewish revolt of 70 AD and Rome's terribly bloody suppression of the Jews for revolting. What is food for thought is underlying implication that if they had repented Heavenly Father would in some way protect them from the worst of the Roman pillaging, burning, and carrying off into slavery that most of the Jewish population experienced. The question becomes to what extent is our faith in God a shield against the trials and tribulations of this life. We all have tragedy. We all have sickness. All of us die. Would it have been worse without our faith or are we singled out for character building oppression because of our faith? I don't know.

16 He that heareth you heareth me; and he that despiseth you despiseth me; and he that despiseth me despiseth him that sent me.
17 **And the seventy returned again with joy, saying, Lord, even the devils are subject unto us through thy name.**
18 **And he said unto them, I beheld Satan as lightning fall from heaven.**

I think "heaven" in this place is not referring to the place where Heavenly Father abides, but the sky above, instead. I do not think that Satan still has access to heaven. That is one of the main reasons I think The Book of Job is not literal, but an allegory. In it we have Satan walking around heaven and having conversations with Heavenly Father. There are other reasons for rejecting that book, but that is one of them.

So I believe what is happening here is Christ is telling the Seventy that their success has been a great frustration to Satan. It is comforting to think that in doing right, we are not only pleasing Heavenly Father, but at the same time frustrating Satan and his plans for us and those we bless in some way. When one kneels down to pray, think about the pleasure you might have in recounting to Heavenly Father that day's victories over Satan.

19 Behold, I give unto you power to tread on serpents and scorpions, and over all the power of the enemy: and nothing shall by any means hurt you.
20 Notwithstanding in this rejoice not, that the spirits are subject unto you; but rather rejoice, because your names are written in heaven.

Another place Christ asks, "What does if profit a man, if he gain the whole world and loose his own soul." It must have been a heady experience for the twelve and the seventy to have the power that Christ gave them when he sent them out to preach. However, we must not let the gifts that Heavenly Father gives us go to our heads. These are just transitory things. Given a commission to do something, Christ also endowed them with the means necessary. When that mission was over, the endowed gifts were withdrawn. That is much like having a Church Calling. Say you are put in charge of the 10 year old boys' Primary Class. Heavenly Father will give you the insights and revelations necessary to teach and lead those boys. However three years later when you have a different calling you would not have the gifts necessary to tell their current leader what to do. You might make suggestions, but gifts that come with the responsibility would be the new leaders. For that reason Christ says not to let those gifts go to your head. Having had a transitory gift means little in the great race of life. What is important is that final goal: Having our names written in heaven. Every thing else is just a means to that end.

21 In that hour Jesus rejoiced in spirit, and said, I thank thee, O Father, Lord of heaven and earth, that thou hast hid these things from the wise and prudent, and hast revealed them unto babes: even so, Father; for so it seemed good in thy sight.

22 All things are delivered to me of my Father: and no man knoweth who the Son is, but the Father; and who the Father is, but the Son, and he to whom the Son will reveal him.

23 **And he turned him unto his disciples, and said privately, Blessed are the eyes which see the things that ye see:**

24 **For I tell you, that many prophets and kings have desired to see those things which ye see, and have not seen them; and to hear those things which ye hear, and have not heard them.**

There are so many many people. It is those of us who have been given the gift of knowing the gospel in this life who are really blessed ones. Think of the millions in autocratic societies where the gospel is not allowed to be preached. Think of the millions born long ago while the gospel was just beginning to spread, and never had a chance to hear. Just think how you have been singled out and rejoice in that.

25 **And, behold, a certain lawyer stood up, and tempted him, saying, Master, what shall I do to inherit eternal life?**

26 **He said unto him, What is written in the law? how readest thou?**

27 **And he answering said, Thou shalt love the Lord thy God with all thy heart, and with all thy soul, and with all thy strength, and with all thy mind; and thy neighbour as thyself.**

28 **And he said unto him, Thou hast answered right: this do, and thou shalt live.**

There are many places in the Scripture where we are given short summations of gospel life presented in a nut shell. My favorite is similar to the above. It is found in the Old Testament, Micah 6:8 which

*Once more it has to be noted that in neither Christ's
conversation with the lawyer nor the Old Testament passage I quoted is
there a list of doctrines that must be espoused, nor a list of rules of
dress, etc. Once again the gospel is way of life. It is a manner of living.
It is expressed in how we live our lives and how we serve our fellow
beings.*

29 **But he, willing to justify himself, said unto Jesus, And who is my
neighbour?**

30 **And Jesus answering said, A certain man went down from
Jerusalem to Jericho, and fell among thieves, which stripped him of
his raiment, and wounded him, and departed, leaving him half
dead.**

31 **And by chance there came down a certain priest that way: and
when he saw him, he passed by on the other side.**

32 **And likewise a Levite, when he was at the place, came and
looked on him, and passed by on the other side.**

33 **But a certain Samaritan, as he journeyed, came where he was:
and when he saw him, he had compassion on him,**

34 **And went to him, and bound up his wounds, pouring in oil and
wine, and set him on his own beast, and brought him to an inn, and
took care of him.**

35 **And on the morrow when he departed, he took out two pence,
and gave them to the host, and said unto him, Take care of him;
and whatsoever thou spendest more, when I come again, I will
repay thee.**

36 **Which now of these three, thinkest thou, was neighbour unto
him that fell among the thieves?**

37 **And he said, He that shewed mercy on him. Then said Jesus**

unto him, Go, and do thou likewise.

Here we have one of the more famous passages of scripture, the Parable of the Good Samaritan. It is hard to shed new light on a passage such as this that has been studied and studied, preached and preached. So, I do not think I will be adding much to the store of knowledge about this section of scripture.

In the story we have a minimum of six people interacting with seventh man who is just going about his business. How are all of these people living the life that has been given them? I see them falling into five groups.

First are the thieves. There are two or more of them, but how many we aren't told. They are just mentioned in the plural. They are our first group. They live their lives preying on their fellow beings. To them, they and theirs are what is important and the rest of us are there to be used and cast aside. They do not have to be lawbreakers to fall into this group. I think the worst of them are lawbreakers of the kind the poor man traveling from Jerusalem to Jericho met. However, there are thieves that work within the law too. This second type thief either takes advantage of our laws or has the laws changed to give himself/herself an advantage that allows them to rob, steal, and take unfair advantage of others. Maybe I am trying to read more into it than is there, but I also think that the fact that Christ says there were more than one of them may have significance too. He may be saying this group is large and there are many of them out there.

The Priest stands for our second group. A priest is a religious leader. He is the one that would be expected to stop and help the poor man who was robbed, beaten and left half dead. Yet this man does not stop and help. He does not even pay much attention to the wounded person, just crosses to the other side of the road to avoid any contact.

Just a Samaritan. Not a member of my congregation, we would not admit him if he asked, he may tell himself and so he is disdainful of the victim. I know lots of people like this.

One of my favorite mottos is the one on the plaque in front of the Statue of Liberty. It says: **"Give me your tired, your poor, your huddled masses yearning to breathe free, the wretched refuse of your teeming shore. Send these, the homeless, tempest-tossed, to me: I lift my lamp beside the golden door."** *What better description can you think of to describe the poor beings fleeing war and strife in the Middle East and Africa. Yet how many of us want that golden door shut in these people's faces. Our society is not perfect, but it is good. One way it got to be good was honoring that motto. We, the richest nation on earth, should be the leader in helping the less fortunate. In many ways we are not, we are the priest passing by on the other side of the road, turning a blind eye to poor wounded wretched masses.*

The Levite stands for our third group. I see him as not the church leader, like the priest, but the church member. He stops, he goes over to look at the poor robbery victim left to die. But who is he? What can he do? He is just a member, not a leader. And, besides he has business in Jericho. Can't be late. He is the man or woman who pays his tithe, puts money into the church, and expects the church to do the good things for him/her. What he/she does not seem to realize is that it could just as easily be him or her lying there in the road. Then they would want and expect help. However, they would not get it. It kinda reminds me of this film clip I saw that showed a school of fish swimming around. Then into their midst drops a fishing line with a hook and worm. One of the fish is tempted and strikes the bait and is hooked. Caught on the line the fish struggles and pulls and jerks trying to get away. It is to no avail and the fish is hauled up and way. What do the other fish do while this is happening. Come to their school mates aid? Flee? No, neither. They just continue their activities like nothing at all was happening. We must not be like those fish or the Levite. We should try to be good neighbors.

Our fourth group is personified in the Good Samaritan who does stop and help and even make provision for the future health of the robbery victim. He does everything right. Enough has been said about this man that I am not sure I can add to the mix.   His actions, though, reflect poorly on many who claim to follow Christ. In our society today, one of the big issues is abortion. Those that oppose it call themselves by the title "Right to Life." It isn't true, however. In most cases it should just be "Right to Birth." They want to save the young child's life but then resist when they are asked to pay for the child's welfare, education, medical expenses, etc. Our good Samaritan not only saves the victim's life, he provides for his care. Abortion is wrong, but so is ignoring the needs of children you save.

Our final person is the innkeeper and the group he represents. I am not sure what is going on here. He helps the poor victim but is paid for his help. There is no "Samaritan you have done enough, let me take over now." He profits from one man's generosity and another's misfortune.

38 Now it came to pass, as they went, that he entered into a certain village: and a certain woman named Martha received him into her house.

39 And she had a sister called Mary, which also sat at Jesus' feet, and heard his word.

40 But Martha was cumbered about much serving, and came to him, and said, Lord, dost thou not care that my sister hath left me to serve alone? bid her therefore that she help me.

41 And Jesus answered and said unto her, Martha, Martha, thou

art careful and troubled about many things:

 42 But one thing is needful: and Mary hath chosen that good part, which shall not be taken away from her.

What a fascinating passage in so many ways. 1st, how typical that the business of taking care of guests falls to the head woman of a house. Such situations were not unique to Christ's time. I have seen it again and again in my home or when visiting other's homes. Most times when this happens the head woman just soldiers on. The meal is half over before she gets to sit down to enjoy the company and food. Others have a good time, and just take the ministrations of that woman for granted. It is her place in life, it is her job, so why notice what she does. She is just doing what is expected. Yet for that woman, doing all the work, it can be hectic. Many times she can feel unappreciated. She can let the workload get her down. In this case I think Martha gives in to such feelings. She lets her frustration boil over and gets mad at her sister, Mary, who is there but who instead of helping serve sits at Jesus feet to listen to him teach.

So many women find themselves in just such situations. They work and slave to make a house a home and get no credit for their efforts, or at least so it seems. Life goes on around them, life they make possible by their efforts, yet what they do goes unnoticed and unappreciated. We should not let such situations exist in our homes.

Now as to Mary, here I am going to make a leap. There are many Marys mentioned in the New Testament. I think the scriptures could be more clear in delineating them for us. There was, of course, the most important Mary, Jesus' Mother. I think the second in importance would be Mary Magdalene. The Magdalene portion of her name just tells us where she is from. It was common in those days to identify a person by their father or the village they lived in. Jesus of Nazareth or Simon bar Jona would be cases in point. Mary lived in

Magdala, another village that lay along the coast of the Sea of Galilee, hence the name Mary Magdalene.

I think there is a good possibility that Mary the sister of Martha is also Mary Magdalene. I say that because of what Jesus says to Martha when she comes to complain about Mary not helping her serve the guests in her home. He told Martha, "She has chosen the good part."

When I read Christ's words "she has chosen the good part" I could not help but think of the story of Ruth in the Old Testament. Let's review it. Naomi, a woman of Bethlehem along with her husband and two sons is forced from their home by famine. They move fifty, to sixty miles to a new home in Moab. There they settle down and the sons marry two local girls. Then tragedy strikes. All three men die. Naomi is left alone with two daughters-in-law. She has nothing and tells the two girls they would be better off if they went back to their families. One does, but the other girl, Ruth, stays with Naomi, telling her "Where you go, I go. And your God will be my God."

In desperation the two women go to Naomi's hometown of Bethlehem. It is harvest time when they arrive. Naomi sends Ruth out to glean (pick up the leftovers) in the fields. In those days the poor were allowed to follow behind the farm workers and gather anything that the workers may have missed. They did not have the mechanical harvesters we have today, and a poor person could gather a good deal of food in this way, maybe even enough to see them through the winter's lean times.

One of Bethlehem's local farmers was a man named Boaz. He sees Ruth gleaning in his fields. Bethlehem was a small village, and the story of Naomi coming back and brining her daughter-in-law with her, and the tragedy the two women had experienced would have been familiar to all. So Boaz tells his farm laborers that are working in front of Ruth to deliberately do a poor job of harvesting, and to leave lots for her to glean.

Ruth is not totally ignorant of what Boaz has done. She could tell stuff was being left for her. When she gets home that evening with lots and lots of food for them, she tells Naomi what happened and Naomi sees an opportunity. That night there would be a big party, Boaz and all his workers would celebrate the harvest by having a big feast and then sleeping in the fields. Naomi tells Ruth to wait till all the men are asleep and then go and uncover Boaz feet, nothing seductive, just pull his blanket back so he feet are exposed. Then she is to lay down there by his feet and go to sleep herself.

Morning comes and Boaz wakes to find his feet uncovered and Ruth there asleep by him. Immediately he takes steps to see if he can claim her to be his wife. To make the story short, he succeeds and marries Ruth. They have a son named Jesse who has a son named David who goes on to be Israel's greatest king and father of the line that Jesus is born into.

Now I do not understand the symbolism at work in the story above. But Naomi and Boaz both did. That uncovering of the feet and then laying there was a signal to him that the woman wanted him. In that culture at that time that is what it meant. I wear a wedding ring. It means and says a lot of things, one being that I am married and not available. I used to go to The Renaissance Faire a lot. There young women would wear a fox tail. It was a symbol that they were looking to hook up with a guy. We have all sorts of ways to send signals in our culture. What Ruth did was a signal in hers.

And so we go back to Martha's house. Mary could have stood against a wall and listened to Christ, she could have found herself a chair, she could have been helping Martha. There are lots of things she could have been doing. But what she did was to sit at Jesus' feet. Now in those days when you went into a home you took your shoes off and left them at the door. You then washed your feet before walking around in the home. So I think the symbolism in Ruth's story and Mary's is the same and that it was not wasted on Jesus. For that reason he tells Martha, "Mary hath chosen that good part, which shall not be taken away from her." Mary wants to do more than just glean truths from Jesus teachings, she wants to be his helpmeet. She wants to be there for him as more than just a disciple.

Did Jesus ever marry? The Catholic Church and most Protestant ones would say no. They believe Jesus did not marry and that is the underpinning of the Catholic doctrine of celibacy of the Priesthood. Since Jesus did not marry, then priests should not either. Protestants have also pretty much said He did not marry. I think in their case there is an underlying, not so much a belief, but at least a feeling, that there is something dirty about sex, even between a husband and wife, and so Jesus would never involve Himself in such. These beliefs are held in spite of the fact that Paul taught that "Marriage is honorable in all, and the bed undefiled."

Paul also taught in Hebrews that: "For we do not have a high priest who is unable to empathize with our weaknesses, but we have one who has been tempted in every way, just as we are--yet he did not sin." A big part of my life is my marriage, and my fatherhood. I am a man, I am a husband, I am a sexual being, and because of those I am a father. Those four things pretty much define me. How can Christ have been tempted in every way, just as I am, and not have experienced them for himself too.

So I am going to take that leap I mentioned above and say yes I believe Jesus married, and I think it was Mary Magdalene He married.

She was probably his most loyal follower, as a spouse should be. When He rose from the dead, who was the first person he appeared to? Mary. And isn't that as it should be if she is his wife? There is a poem about her that goes:

Not she with traitorous kiss her Master stung,

Not she denied Him with unfaithful tongue;

She, when Apostles fled, could dangers brave,

Last at the Cross, and earliest at the grave.

I am not sure where this will be added. I have been thinking about things and it has a occurred to me that the protestant and catholic churches are much like modern science. (It may be a western civilization thing, an attribute of our cultural, that results in a desire to have everything fit neatly into a box. Eastern religions, even eastern Christianity does not seem so fixated on everything being logical and "faithful." They rely on tradition and ritual.) Science has rejected the idea of a god. Or at least a god that takes an active hand in the universe's affairs. They are forced into this position because God is a wild card that can change any equation. These scientists can burn oxygen and hydrogen and make water consistently. There are rules and they discover them, and follow them and voila, water. Christ (read God) however, can make water into wine. That is not possible says the scientist. The requisite atoms are not there for the transformation. It follows, therefore, Christ did not exist, or if he did stories were made up about him. Miracles violate the rules and must be rejected to keep everything neat and orderly.

Western religion, like western science, also wants everything to fit nicely together. In order to make this happen they say that when John put a period at the end of the last sentence of his Book of

Revelation, that God quit giving revelations, that He quit speaking to man, that the Bible is all there is and it is enough, we need nothing more. The only need is for theologians, and pastors and teachers to tell us what the Bible teaches. But now, along comes Mormonism and says God still speaks, and there are prophets through which He does so. To Western Christanity the whole concept of modern day prophets is to open the door to a wild card. Just as the scientist thinks of God, so the Protestant and Catholic church think of prophets, and so they oppose the idea.

Each in their own way wants everything tied up neatly in brown paper with nice string bow holding it all together. Life, however, is not that way.

I am sure I will write more on this.

I entered and internet discussion on a verse that spoke of enduring to the end and I remarked that it did not sound like "Once saved, always saved." Later I got to thinking that the once saved always saved idea is much like Tetzel, and the mistaken idea that you could buy an "indulgence" that would forgive all your sins, past, present, and future.

1 And it came to pass, that, as he was praying in a certain place, when he ceased, one of his disciples said unto him, Lord, teach us to pray, as John also taught his disciples.

2 And he said unto them, When ye pray, say, Our Father which art in heaven, Hallowed be thy name. Thy kingdom come. Thy will be done, as in heaven, so in earth.

3 Give us day by day our daily bread.

4 And forgive us our sins; for we also forgive every one that is indebted to us. And lead us not into temptation; but deliver us from evil.

So much has been written on the Lord's Prayer, I can't think of a single new insight to offer. If something comes to me I will add it later.

5 And he said unto them, Which of you shall have a friend, and shall go unto him at midnight, and say unto him, Friend, lend me three loaves;

6 For a friend of mine in his journey is come to me, and I have nothing to set before him?

7 And he from within shall answer and say, Trouble me not: the door is now shut, and my children are with me in bed; I cannot rise and give thee.

8 I say unto you, Though he will not rise and give him, because he is his friend, yet because of his importunity he will rise and give him as many as he needeth.

9 And I say unto you, Ask, and it shall be given you; seek, and ye shall find; knock, and it shall be opened unto you.

10 For every one that asketh receiveth; and he that seeketh findeth; and to him that knocketh it shall be opened.

11 If a son shall ask bread of any of you that is a father, will he give him a stone? or if he ask a fish, will he for a fish give him a serpent?

12 Or if he shall ask an egg, will he offer him a scorpion?

13 If ye then, being evil, know how to give good gifts unto your children: how much more shall your heavenly Father give the Holy Spirit to them that ask him?

Although Christ is speaking in broad terms here, I believe the application is more narrow. Christ says it in one way as we find above, James, in his epistle says it another: " If any of you lack wisdom, let him ask of God, that giveth to all men liberally, and upbraideth not; and it shall be given him." That is James 1:5.

I do not think Christ is speaking of just anything here. He is not saying if you want to be rich, ask. If you want to be smart, ask. If you want to be a sports star, ask. If you want a missing tooth to grow back, ask, etc. James sort of narrows it down for us. Heavenly Father is offering us wisdom, spiritual insight, understanding, in other words, the gifts of the spirit.

We are speaking here of the Holy Spirit coming into God's children's lives and the wisdom he will bestow on those children if they ask. I would note that the only requirement in both Luke's gospel and James epistle is asking. That is the single qualification. A PhD in Theology is not a prerequisite. Having memorized a set of doctrines is not a prerequisite. Being an adult is not a prerequisite. Being a male is not a prerequisite. Just asking, that is all.

God spoke to the child, Samuel. God spoke to the teenaged boy, Joseph. God spoke to the young adult, Mary. God spoke to the middle aged Paul. God spoke to the elderly Anna. In only one of the these cases are we told they specifically asked, but I think it is safe to assume they all asked, and they all were answered.

So then, what Christ is teaching us is: Don't understand a passage in the Bible? Don't know what to do in a situation? Ask and you will get the wisdom to understand.

14 And he was casting out a devil, and it was dumb. And it came to pass, when the devil was gone out, the dumb spake; and the people wondered.

It would seem that whomever had this devil could not speak because the demon could not speak, or possibly this demon's form of possession was to render the person under its influence unable to speak. I am not sure it is important to worry about which of these explanations is correct either. I find that worrying about demons, studying them, etc is unprofitable. They exist. The more you worry about them and fixate on them, the more they can rob you of spiritual strength.

15 But some of them said, He casteth out devils through Beelzebub the chief of the devils.

16 And others, tempting him, sought of him a sign from heaven.

17 But he, knowing their thoughts, said unto them, Every kingdom divided against itself is brought to desolation; and a house divided against a house falleth.

18 If Satan also be divided against himself, how shall his kingdom stand? because ye say that I cast out devils through Beelzebub.

19 And if I by Beelzebub cast out devils, by whom do your sons cast them out? therefore shall they be your judges.

20 But if I with the finger of God cast out devils, no doubt the kingdom of God is come upon you.

21 When a strong man armed keepeth his palace, his goods are in peace:

22 But when a stronger than he shall come upon him, and overcome him, he taketh from him all his armour wherein he trusted, and divideth his spoils.

Now comes a series of unrelated anecdotes.

23 He that is not with me is against me: and he that gathereth not with me scattereth.

You can be part of building God's Kingdom or you can get in the way and hinder the construction. Christ does not allow for any middle ground.

24 When the unclean spirit is gone out of a man, he walketh through dry places, seeking rest; and finding none, he saith, I will return unto my house whence I came out.

25 And when he cometh, he findeth it swept and garnished.

26 Then goeth he, and taketh to him seven other spirits more wicked than himself; and they enter in, and dwell there: and the last state of that man is worse than the first.

The cast out spirit finds itself in a restless and dry place. Unhappy there it wants to get back into the person from whom it was cast out. The person, however, has made an effort to get their life in order. While it is not stated, that person's efforts at remaking their lives in a neat and orderly manner seem to protect them from being repossessed. However the person's efforts are not proof against a herd of demons and they are again taken over. As a result, Christ says the man is now worse than before.

Now Christ went around casting out devils. Why would He do this if those He was supposedly helping were worse off a few days later. There has to be more here than is stated. We have to read between the lines. Here is what I find there: Christ was busy establishing His church. It was a sanctuary where among other things there was "deliverance to the captives" (Luke 4:18) as we heard when He started His ministry and told to whom He was going. I think that within the arms of His church there the former possessed person can be safe from the demon that once possessed them, even if it brings some other demons along in an effort to take the person back over.

Sadly, I think the man who lost out to the hoard of demons was trying to do things on his own. If he had had the power of Christ's church standing with him he would have prevailed. Church membership and the companionship of other believers is a powerful weapon in our personal armor. United we stand, divided we fall is true of our spiritual lives too.

27 And it came to pass, as he spake these things, a certain woman of the company lifted up her voice, and said unto him, Blessed is the womb that bare thee, and the paps which thou hast sucked.
28 But he said, Yea rather, blessed are they that hear the word of God, and keep it.

It is all about life style. He does not say blessed are the _______ and you can fill in that blank with all the things the modern church equates with godliness. You can try words like bishops, theologians, tithe payers, television evangelists, deacons, priests, elders, Sunday school teachers, wives, mothers, fathers, etc. The list goes on. You can stick any of those words in, but they would be wrong. Christ tells us the blank should be filled with "they that hear the word of God, and keep it." Now a bishop can hear the word of God and keep it, and thus earn the designation: BLESSED. But he does not get to be blessed by being a bishop. They get that by hearing and keeping God's word, and that hearing and keeping can then result in them being a bishop. But to be blessed, they must first hear and keep. The other offices and/or blessings come in Christ's true church to those who hear and keep the word.

As for hearing and keeping God's word, some of us will know more of it and others less. What is important is the keeping of what we have been privileged to hear. We find an example in the Book of Acts. In chapter 19 we read:

1And it came to pass, that, while Apollos was at Corinth, Paul having passed through the upper coasts came to Ephesus: and finding certain disciples,

2 He said unto them, Have ye received the Holy Ghost since ye believed? And they said unto him, We have not so much as heard whether there be any Holy Ghost. (Obviously not Trinitarians, so are they lost hell bound sinners? I believe not. They are following the light and knowledge they have and Heavenly Father will honor that.)

3 And he said unto them, Unto what then were ye baptized? And they said, Unto John's baptism.

4 Then said Paul, John verily baptized with the baptism of repentance, saying unto the people, that they should believe on him which should come after him, that is, on Christ Jesus.

5 When they heard this, they were baptized in the name of the Lord Jesus.

6 And when Paul had laid his hands upon them, the Holy Ghost came on them; and they spake with tongues, and prophesied.

I need to find a way to work this in some how. These people are John's disciples. Good people. Just not having the full gospel. They are not lost, just doing the best they can with what light they see.

One of my favorite men, Thomas Monson, our Prophet, died a few years ago. The article I read concerning him and his passing (which I believe would mostly be written by the church and passed on to the press in hopes they might use portions of it) quoted a Professor Mauss of Washington State University as saying, "President Monson always seemed more interested in what we do with our religion rather than in what we believed."

I fear that, unlike Paul, pride in some church members is often quick to condemn other believers that don't have the depth of knowledge they have. Some would even consign them to hell for their lack of knowledge or misunderstanding of some doctrine or another. I feel otherwise. I believe Heavenly Father will honor his children that are true to the light and knowledge they have been given. Many times he will send a Paul to further enlighten them, but such is not always the case. As for Heavenly Father, I think He is more interested in what we do with our religion rather than what we believe.

And what of those that are true and faithful to the light they have been given but die before hearing the whole truth? My guess it is people like them that Paul had in mind in 1st Cor. 15 verse 29 when he said, "Else what shall they do which are baptized for the dead, if the dead rise not at all? why are they then baptized for the dead?" People who were and would be open to the truth if they heard it, they deserve this second chance.

29 And when the people were gathered thick together, he began to say, This is an evil generation: they seek a sign; and there shall no sign be given it, but the sign of Jonas the prophet.
30 For as Jonas was a sign unto the Ninevites, so shall also the Son

of man be to this generation.

31 **The queen of the south shall rise up in the judgment with the men of this generation, and condemn them: for she came from the utmost parts of the earth to hear the wisdom of Solomon; and, behold, a greater than Solomon is here.**

32 **The men of Nineve shall rise up in the judgment with this generation, and shall condemn it: for they repented at the preaching of Jonas; and, behold, a greater than Jonas is here.**

The circus is coming to town. There will be all sorts of amazing things to see. People drop what they are doing and crowd around to see and experience the strangeness. I think that is what is happening here. They, at least the majority of these people, have come to see a miracle. This angers Christ and he condemns them for wanting to see a show instead of hear the gospel. Their souls hang in the balance and yet they opt for glitz and glamour instead help leading a righteous life.

We are to be judged by our righteousness, our repentance, our atonement and not some belief system.

We live in a special age. So much knowledge is available to us through books, television, the internet, etc. that I believe we are going to be held to a very high standard as pertains to our relationship with the truth. As we just commented on, Christ said "seek and ye shall find." Those that came before us had a much harder time in their seeking. They did not have the truth available to them so easily and quickly. These facts reduce our ability to use ignorance as an excuse.

33 **No man, when he hath lighted a candle, putteth it in a secret place, neither under a bushel, but on a candlestick, that they which come in may see the light.**

We have the light that a darkened world needs. There is a lot of darkness on the internet, and elsewhere in life we find political darkness, religious darkness, sexual darkness, and the darkness of ignorance, they all abound. But there is a candle burning in the midst of that darkness too. It is the candle of the gospel. People that come to that light can find forgiveness, they can find purpose, they can find reason.

34 The light of the body is the eye: therefore when thine eye is single, thy whole body also is full of light; but when thine eye is evil, thy body also is full of darkness.

I am not sure what Christ had in mind for His day and age, but for ours, I think pornography fits the bill. It is a way to fill the body with darkness.

35 Take heed therefore that the light which is in thee be not darkness.
36 If thy whole body therefore be full of light, having no part dark, the whole shall be full of light, as when the bright shining of a candle doth give thee light.
37 And as he spake, a certain Pharisee besought him to dine with him: and he went in, and sat down to meat.
38 And when the Pharisee saw it, he marvelled that he had not first washed before dinner.
39 And the Lord said unto him, Now do ye Pharisees make clean the outside of the cup and the platter; but your inward part is full of ravening and wickedness.
40 Ye fools, did not he that made that which is without make that which is within also?

41 **But rather give alms of such things as ye have; and, behold, all things are clean unto you.**
42 **But woe unto you, Pharisees! for ye tithe mint and rue and all manner of herbs, and pass over judgment and the love of God: these ought ye to have done, and not to leave the other undone.**

43 Woe unto you, Pharisees! for ye love the uppermost seats in the synagogues, and greetings in the markets.

44 Woe unto you, scribes and Pharisees, hypocrites! for ye are as graves which appear not, and the men that walk over them are not aware of them.

Christ does not condemn their good works. He just says they are not enough. They also need the "Love of God." Once filled with love they will not spend their days in judgment of others. They will no longer want the best seats in the synagogue for themselves, etc.

It would seem that the Jews had an aversion to walking on graves. I am not sure why.

45 Then answered one of the lawyers, and said unto him, Master, thus saying thou reproachest us also.

46 And he said, Woe unto you also, ye lawyers! for ye lade men with burdens grievous to be borne, and ye yourselves touch not the burdens with one of your fingers.

47 Woe unto you! for ye build the sepulchres of the prophets, and your fathers killed them.

48 Truly ye bear witness that ye allow the deeds of your fathers: for they indeed killed them, and ye build their sepulchres.

This reminds me of current politicians that pass laws for the common folk to keep, but exempt themselves from these same laws.

How often do we make excuses for earlier generations and their sins, saying they just didn't know any better. We see our generation as enlightened and those that came before as blighted. Maybe in those "good old days" there were a few "prophets" that stood up and said this and that was wrong. These prophets were ahead of their times, and were persecuted for their stand against evil. Now we as a people have come around to those enlightened views, but we do not condemn our forbearers.

49 Therefore also said the wisdom of God, I will send them prophets and apostles, and some of them they shall slay and persecute:
50 **That the blood of all the prophets, which was shed from the foundation of the world, may be required of this generation;**
51 **From the blood of Abel unto the blood of Zacharias, which perished between the altar and the temple: verily I say unto you, It shall be required of this generation.**

This is a passage about which I wonder what Jesus is talking about. His audience is Jewish people and He does not tell a long tale, instead He calls to their minds things that they should be knowledgeable of.

First He mentions Able. The Bible does not tell us much about Able, just that he was the son of Adam and Eve and that Heavenly Father accepted his sacrifice but rejected his brother Cain's, and for that reason Cain killed Able. We have no other scriptures telling us more about Able and the life he lived before being murdered, but here comes Christ and calls him a prophet. In doing so He opens a window that lets in some light where Able is concerned, we can now bank on the fact that Able must have been a righteous man who communed with God.

Both myself and I would guess most of my readers, however, are ignorant of what He is referring to, at least so far as Zacharias is concerned. We know of the birth of Zacharias' son, John the Baptist, because it is told in the beginning of the gospel of Luke and we have already discussed it. We are told that Zacharias perished between the altar and the temple but not how or why. The way Christ speaks of

Zacharias death without elaboration, it would seem He expects His listeners to be familiar with the story and how it happened. However, what was common knowledge in Christ's time in Palestine has been lost these two millennia later.

One of the rules I laid down for myself in writing this commentary on the Book of Luke was that I would present readers with my views on what I read and wrote about. I would provide my views, and only rarely look elsewhere for help. I have kept that rule. I want the spiritual viewpoints found in here to be my own. However, I think I can be true to that rule and seek help on this passage because I am looking for not spiritual insight, but instead historical understanding.

There is a source of further detail it the traditions of The Eastern Orthodox Church. Whether this tradition is true or not, I could not say. It does however, answer questions about verse 51. The tradition goes as follows:

When Jesus was born in Bethlehem and the Magi came from the East, they told Herod of the newborn king. Herod sent soldiers to slay all the children in Bethlehem, and remembering John, for he had been informed of all that had occurred at John's birth, since everyone who lived in the country spoke of the wonder, Herod laid up all he had in his heart concerning John, saying, "What manner of child shall this be? Will this child be the King of the Jews?" He decided to kill John to and sent executioners to Zacharias' house. The executioners did not find John there and the slaughter of children began. When Elizabeth heard these cries and the reason for them, she took John and fled into the mountains. At this time Zacharias was serving as a priest in Jerusalem. When Elizabeth saw soldiers drawing near, she prayed to God and cried out to the rocky mount nearby and said, "O mountain of God, receive a mother and her child!" Immediately the mountain was split and she entered hiding herself and John from the executioners. The soldiers returned to Herod, having not found the child, and Herod sent word to Zacharias in the temple saying, " Surrender your son John to me." Saint Zacharias replied, "I serve the Lord God of Israel. As for my son, I do not know where he is."

Herod was enraged and sent word to Zacharias again ordering that he be killed if he did not surrender his son. The executioners made haste and demanded of Zacharias, "Where have you hidden your son? Give him to us and obey the King's command! If you do not give us your son, you shall be put to death immediately." Saint Zacharias replied, "You will kill my body, but the Lord will receive my soul." The executioners straightway fulfilled Herod's command and fell upon Zacharias between the temple and the altar. His blood was spilt on the floor and became hardened like rock as a testimony against Herod and a witness to his eternal condemnation.

So there we have a possible explanation of the circumstances surrounding Zacharias' death which Jesus mentions as being between the temple and the altar.

52 Woe unto you, lawyers! for ye have taken away the key of knowledge: ye entered not in yourselves, and them that were entering in ye hindered.

53 And as he said these things unto them, the scribes and the Pharisees began to urge him vehemently, and to provoke him to speak of many things:

54 Laying wait for him, and seeking to catch something out of his mouth, that they might accuse him.

Chapter 12

1 In the mean time, when there were gathered together an innumerable multitude of people, insomuch that they trode one upon another, he began to say unto his disciples first of all, Beware ye of the leaven of the Pharisees, which is hypocrisy.

2 For there is nothing covered, that shall not be revealed; neither hid, that shall not be known.

3 Therefore whatsoever ye have spoken in darkness shall be heard in the light; and that which ye have spoken in the ear in closets shall be proclaimed upon the housetops.

4 And I say unto you my friends, Be not afraid of them that kill the body, and after that have no more that they can do.

5 But I will forewarn you whom ye shall fear: Fear him, which after he hath killed hath power to cast into hell; yea, I say unto you, Fear him.

6 **Are not five sparrows sold for two farthings, and not one of them is forgotten before God?**

7 **But even the very hairs of your head are all numbered. Fear not therefore: ye are of more value than many sparrows.**

It is such a comfort to know that Heavenly Father has His eye on us. In the midst of pain, suffering, indecision, ignorance and all our many failings God is watching over us.

8 Also I say unto you, Whosoever shall confess me before men, him shall the Son of man also confess before the angels of God:

9 But he that denieth me before men shall be denied before the angels of God.

10 **And whosoever shall speak a word against the Son of man, it shall be forgiven him: but unto him that blasphemeth against the**

Holy Ghost it shall not be forgiven.

That is a verse I do not understand. Why is one worse than the other. Why do we set up a ranking of sins? Yes, I can see where thievery and mayhem and murder are worse than some minor sin. The Catholics have venial and mortal sins. The mortal will send you to hell, the venial will require some working off in purgatory. Most people seem to see sexual sins as the worst, but are they? I think sins against children should be seen as the worst. Other's, I guess, would have a different opinion. Whatever, sin is wrong and we need to abhor it in all its forms.

11   And when they bring you unto the synagogues, and unto magistrates, and powers, take ye no thought how or what thing ye shall answer, or what ye shall say:
12   For the Holy Ghost shall teach you in the same hour what ye ought to say.
13   And one of the company said unto him, Master, speak to my brother, that he divide the inheritance with me.
14   And he said unto him, Man, who made me a judge or a divider over you?
15   **And he said unto them, Take heed, and beware of covetousness: for a man's life consisteth not in the abundance of the things which he possesseth.**

Usually wealth is acquired through someone else's loss. This is not always the case, but I would venture a guess that it is true of the vast majority of wealth the rich aquire. A man or woman sees what others have and desires these things for themselves too. To get them, however, someone else has to be exploited. The desire to have overcomes the basic humanity of an individual and they climb over others in their attempt to get riches and what riches will allow them to acquire. No wonder that elsewhere Christ said it is harder for a camel to pass through the eye of the needle than for a rich man to enter heaven. (Literal reading of that in our modern terms makes it impossible for a rich man to go to heaven. However, Christ lived in the day of walled cities with heavy wooden gates to keep out enemies. During the day an opposing army could be seen coming and the gates closed. At night the bad guys could approach under the cover of darkness and run through the gate before the city guards could react and close the gate. As a result the gate was always closed in the evening, precluding a sneak attack. However, people could not always time their arrivals to the daytime. To allow for this a small door like affair could be opened and closed after dark to allow these late arrivals a way in. This entrance was always small and easily defended. It was called the "eye of the needle" because of its size. A person could get through, but if they showed up on a camel it was very hard for the animal to get through the mansized entrance. The camel would need to be stripped of all it was carrying and get down on its knees and lower its head and squeeze through. A very difficult task and hence Christ's saying about a rich man getting into heaven being harder than getting a camel into the city after dark.

16 **And he spake a parable unto them, saying, The ground of a certain rich man brought forth plentifully:**

17 **And he thought within himself, saying, What shall I do, because I have no room where to bestow my fruits?**

18 **And he said, This will I do: I will pull down my barns, and build greater; and there will I bestow all my fruits and my goods.**

19 **And I will say to my soul, Soul, thou hast much goods laid up for many years; take thine ease, eat, drink, and be merry.**

20 **But God said unto him, Thou fool, this night thy soul shall be required of thee: then whose shall those things be, which thou hast provided?**

21 **So is he that layeth up treasure for himself, and is not rich toward God.**

And again Christ takes up the subject of being rich. He once more speaks out against wealth. Instead of hoarding his riches the man should have made points with Heavenly Father by helping others who did not have as much. Then when he stood at the judgment seat he might have received that mercy he denied others. How often do we ignore opportunities to share what has been given to us. This is true of us as individuals and as a country too. Our Statue of Liberty has a motto that would gain us much favor with Heavenly Father if we lived up to it, but the national mood sees to run contrary to it. As a reminder the motto is:

<u>Give me your tired, your poor, Your huddled masses yearning to breathe free, The wretched refuse of your teeming shore. Send these, the homeless, tempest-tossed to me, I lift my lamp beside the golden door!</u>

22 And he said unto his disciples, Therefore I say unto you, Take no thought for your life, what ye shall eat; neither for the body, what ye shall put on.

23 The life is more than meat, and the body is more than raiment.

Notice that He does not say that food and clothes are not important, just that life is so much more. It is not important that we live this phase of our existence in comfort. This is not a time to luxuriate. It is a time to learn, to serve, and to grow spiritually. How did Peter say to spend our time? "Add to your faith virtue, and to virtue knowledge, and knowledge temperance, and to temperance patience, and to patience brotherly kindness, and to brotherly kindness charity (re: love)."

I would point out that Peter lists seven things. Knowledge, which I would consider the study of doctrine is just one of them and it does not come first either. Too many Christians get hung up on doctrinal studies to the exclusion or near exclusion of the other six things Peter tells us to do. Do not be one of them. What you do with your religion is so much more important than the nuances of your beliefs concerning some arcane doctrine. Paul told the Corinthians "For I determined to know nothing among you save Jesus Christ and Him crucified."

Something else to think on. In Peter's list he follows Knowledge with Temperance which means moderation or self-control. He could have listed his seven qualities in any order. However, he chose to follow knowledge, which I interpret to be doctrinal studies, with a call for moderation and self-control. Historically Christians have fought wars over different doctrines, such as the Trinity, the Lord's Supper, etc. Thankfully we are no longer killing each other over doctrine.

Today many Christians just disassociate themselves from those who read some scripture verse differently. They then spend their time studying doctrine in the attempt to find more reasons to condemn those who see things differently. This is not the moderation Peter is calling for. All that time spent disproving someone else's doctrine you could instead be adding to your faith, virtue, brotherly kindness, patience, and charity. We should not let ideas and doctrines get in the way of doing good. A system of beliefs is not the core of Christianity, it is how we live our lives that counts. James said, "Pure religion and undefiled before God and the Father is this, To visit the fatherless and widows in their affliction, and to keep himself unspotted from the world." It is lifestyle, folks, lifestyle, not a PhD is doctrine that is going to stand us in good stead when the books are opened and we are judged.

Here is a little something more. Today's Sunday school lesson dealt with when Israel was in the wilderness and Moses sends 12 spies into the Promised Land to check it out prior to the Israelites' invasion into the land that God had promised them. When they came back all the spies agreed it was a land flowing with milk and honey. One bunch of grapes they returned with took two men to carry it. However, while Caleb and Joshua agreed they should go in and take the land promised them, the other ten spies said the people were too strong and would easily defeat and kill them if they tried. The people sided with the ten spies and refuse to invade the land. This angered God and He said they (with the exception of Caleb and Joshua) would have to wander in the wilderness forty more years, until all the adults alive at that time had died, then the next generation would get a chance to go in and take the land.

That, of course is an interesting and well known story from the scriptures. Here is the thought I had while we were discussing it in class. When Israel refused to invade they were south of the Holy Land, on the west side of the Dead Sea. If they entered the land from that direction one of the first people they would have encountered and had to deal with would have been the Philistines. If they had done so, at this point when they were at peak strength they would have conquered them and how different their history would have been. The Philistines became their worst enemy. They were a constant problem. Goliath was a Philistine. King Saul was killed by them. Samson. The list goes on.

Instead they wander forty years in the wilderness and when they do invade they do so across the Jordon River to attack Jericho. They conquer the mountainous area of Palestine, but not the plains by the sea where the Philistines lived. The sin of that first generation haunted their children and grandchildren and so on for generations.

24 Consider the ravens: for they neither sow nor reap; which neither have storehouse nor barn; and God feedeth them: how much more are ye better than the fowls?

25 And which of you with taking thought can add to his stature one cubit?

26 If ye then be not able to do that thing which is least, why take ye thought for the rest?

27 Consider the lilies how they grow: they toil not, they spin not; and yet I say unto you, that Solomon in all his glory was not arrayed like one of these.

28 If then God so clothe the grass, which is to day in the field, and to morrow is cast into the oven; how much more will he clothe you, O ye of little faith.

29 And seek not ye what ye shall eat, or what ye shall drink, neither be ye of doubtful mind.

30 For all these things do the nations of the world seek after: and your Father knoweth that ye have need of these things.

31 But rather seek ye the kingdom of God; and all these things shall be added unto you.

32 Fear not, little flock; for it is your Father's good pleasure to give you the kingdom.

33 Sell that ye have, and give alms; provide yourselves bags which wax not old, a treasure in the heavens that faileth not, where no thief approacheth, neither moth corrupteth.

34 **For where your treasure is, there will your heart be also.**

Christ is so correct in this statement. It is a short verse, just eleven words, but they say so much. If you value heaven and your future life there, you will put your heart into doing good here in this life. You will devote your time and energies helping others. You may not be a Reverend, but you will be a minister.

35 Let your loins be girded about, and your lights burning;

36 And ye yourselves like unto men that wait for their lord, when he will return from the wedding; that when he cometh and knocketh, they may open unto him immediately.

37 Blessed are those servants, whom the lord when he cometh shall find watching: verily I say unto you, that he shall gird himself, and make them to sit down to meat, and will come forth and serve them.

38 And if he shall come in the second watch, or come in the third watch, and find them so, blessed are those servants.

39 And this know, that if the goodman of the house had known what hour the thief would come, he would have watched, and not have suffered his house to be broken through.

40 **Be ye therefore ready also: for the Son of man cometh at an hour when ye think not.**

So many have come along and claimed to have found some secret that allows them to know when Jesus will return. Every date they have set has failed. We do not know when He will come. The apostle Paul looked for it to happen in his lifetime and it didn't. Others have gone to their grave equally disappointed. Rather than try to set a date to be ready, just be ready. If He comes and you are ready you are in good shape. If you are ready and He does not come, you are still in good shape.

41 Then Peter said unto him, Lord, speakest thou this parable unto us, or even to all?

42 And the Lord said, Who then is that faithful and wise steward, whom his lord shall make ruler over his household, to give them their portion of meat in due season?

43 **Blessed is that servant, whom his lord when he cometh shall find so doing.**

No one knows when the Lord will come again. The trick is to be prepared for it. Be packed and ready to go. You don't want to be doing something so that you find yourself saying, "Uh-oh" when that light shines out of the east and unto the west to announce Christ's return. If I could use a cartoon as illustration, please. It one of my favorites and it *shows an older white haired gentleman in a white suit standing before a gate. On each side of the gate is a giant statue of a chicken. The gate itself is of wrought iron and it too displays chickens. The man is saying, "Uh-oh." The title of the cartoon is entitled: <u>Colonel Sanders at the Pearly Gates</u>.*

We need to prepare for our meeting with Saint Peter at the pearly gates by caring about the things he cares about. And what is that? We learn in the Temple the behaviors Heavenly Father wants and make promises or covenants to do so. It is the keeping of those covenants that will see us welcomed to God's Kingdom. Should we be alive at Christ's 2nd coming it is the keeping of those same covenants that will caught up to meet Him.

44 Of a truth I say unto you, that he will make him ruler over all that he hath.

45 But and if that servant say in his heart, My lord delayeth his coming; and shall begin to beat the menservants and maidens, and to eat and drink, and to be drunken;

46 **The lord of that servant will come in a day when he looketh not for him, and at an hour when he is not aware, and will cut him in sunder, and will appoint him his portion with the unbelievers.**

It is important to be about our master's work, doing the things He taught us. Those that fail at this will be left behind.

47 And that servant, which knew his lord's will, and prepared not himself, neither did according to his will, shall be beaten with many stripes.

48 **But he that knew not, and did commit things worthy of stripes, shall be beaten with few stripes. For unto whomsoever much is given, of him shall be much required: and to whom men have committed much, of him they will ask the more.**

Living as we do in a age where the gospel is widely disseminated unbelievers have much less excuse and their pleas of ignorance will ring hollow in many cases.

This present age gives a man or woman so many more opportunities to be good and/or to be bad than I think they had in earlier times. For that reason, God will expect more of us. We must be better than those that came before. I read often of Jesus disciples and wonder how they can be so dumb sometimes. They actually physically walked with Christ on a daily basis and yet they do and ask these ignorant questions. But we must not forget they did not have the New Testament yet, nor the Holy Spirit. We know how things were going to end, they didn't. They can plead their ignorance; we have no excuse.

Now for another insert that may find its way into to this commentary. I was in Sunday School this past week and we are studying the Old Testament. At this time, we are looking at the kings of Israel and Judah and the prophets Heavenly Father sent to warn them of their sins. What stood out to me is that the prophets were pretty ineffective in their attempts to lead God's people to live a spiritual life. However, when a righteous king was on the throne the people lived much more god-fearing lives. The prophets were beating their heads against a wall, but a king had the power and leadership to lead his people to live virtuous lives. I think that translates into our lives too. We have elected a President who is a compulsive liar, a serial adulterer, and a blasphemer and he deliberately has made our society much more divided. Good people who strive after righteousness have a wedge driven between them because of his divisive presence.

49 I am come to send fire on the earth; and what will I if it be already kindled?

50 But I have a baptism to be baptized with; and how am I straitened till it be accomplished!

51 Suppose ye that I am come to give peace on earth? I tell you, Nay; but rather division:

52 For from henceforth there shall be five in one house divided, three against two, and two against three.

53 The father shall be divided against the son, and the son against the father; the mother against the daughter, and the daughter against the mother; the mother in law against her daughter in law, and the daughter in law against her mother in law.

54 And he said also to the people, When ye see a cloud rise out of the west, straightway ye say, There cometh a shower; and so it is.

55 And when ye see the south wind blow, ye say, There will be heat; and it cometh to pass.

56 Ye hypocrites, ye can discern the face of the sky and of the earth; but how is it that ye do not discern this time?

57 Yea, and why even of yourselves judge ye not what is right?

58 When thou goest with thine adversary to the magistrate, as thou art in the way, give diligence that thou mayest be delivered from him; lest he hale thee to the judge, and the judge deliver thee to the officer, and the officer cast thee into prison.

59 I tell thee, thou shalt not depart thence, till thou hast paid the very last mite.

Chapter 13

1 **There were present at that season some that told him of the Galilaeans, whose blood Pilate had mingled with their sacrifices.**
2 **And Jesus answering said unto them, Suppose ye that these Galilaeans were sinners above all the Galilaeans, because they suffered such things?**
3 **I tell you, Nay: but, except ye repent, ye shall all likewise perish.**
4 **Or those eighteen, upon whom the tower in Siloam fell, and slew them, think ye that they were sinners above all men that dwelt in Jerusalem?**
5 **I tell you, Nay: but, except ye repent, ye shall all likewise perish.**

We live in a world where bad things happen, and they happen to the good and the bad people. Some years ago I was watching a televangelist on TV and he was blaming our government for a hurricane that came ashore in Virginia. If we had had a good God-fearing government the hurricane would not have happened or would have gone someplace else. Such was his message. That does not seem to be the message of this passage. We all need to repent. And even when we do, bad things will still happen.

I am 73 and my wife just turned 72. Someday one of us is going to die and leave the other alone to face this life. That is bad, but it is the human condition. What we must do is as the Savior says, repent and bring forth the fruits of that repentance in our lives. Then when this world's tragedies over take us we can face them knowing our eternity is secured.

6 He spake also this parable; A certain man had a fig tree planted in his vineyard; and he came and sought fruit thereon, and found none.

7 Then said he unto the dresser of his vineyard, Behold, these three years I come seeking fruit on this fig tree, and find none: cut it down; why cumbereth it the ground?

8 And he answering said unto him, Lord, let it alone this year also, till I shall dig about it, and dung it:

9 And if it bear fruit, well: and if not, then after that thou shalt cut it down.

10 And he was teaching in one of the synagogues on the sabbath.

11 And, behold, there was a woman which had a spirit of infirmity eighteen years, and was bowed together, and could in no wise lift up herself.

12 And when Jesus saw her, he called her to him, and said unto her, Woman, thou art loosed from thine infirmity.

13 And he laid his hands on her: and immediately she was made straight, and glorified God.

14 And the ruler of the synagogue answered with indignation, because that Jesus had healed on the sabbath day, and said unto the people, There are six days in which men ought to work: in them therefore come and be healed, and not on the sabbath day.

15 The Lord then answered him, and said, Thou hypocrite, doth not each one of you on the sabbath loose his ox or his ass from the stall, and lead him away to watering?

16 And ought not this woman, being a daughter of Abraham, whom Satan hath bound, lo, these eighteen years, be loosed from this bond on the sabbath day?

17 And when he had said these things, all his adversaries were ashamed: and all the people rejoiced for all the glorious things that were done by him.

The people of Israel were very strict in their rules as to what could be done of the Sabbath. They are not alone in this, just probably the most severe in their rules. Many modern Christian Churches have their rules too. I am not aware but would not be surprised to learn that Muslims also have similar strictures. Jesus found these practices wrong and a careful reading of this passage and others like it will give you the impression that He went out of his way to stir things up by deliberately healing people on the sabbath.

Having a rigid set of rules can get groups into trouble. No or zero tolerance can sound like a good idea until it is put into practice. I can remember where a school district, in answer to a school shooting some place in the country developed a zero-tolerance policy where guns or even play guns brought on campus would result in expulsion of the student that violated it. Well, I image that sounded like a good idea when children are being shot by other children on campus. Rightfully so, they wanted to do something to make sure nothing like that occurred on one of their campuses. But then, one day, a child brought a rifle to school. It was just a toy rifle, in fact, it was the rifle from the child's toy soldier. The kind of toy soldier comes in a bag of toy soldiers, the kind of toy soldier that is made out of plastic and stands about three inches tall, the kind of toy soldier that has a rifle that is about two inches long. The school district was made to look foolish when they strictly interpreted their zero tolerance policy and kicked the child out of school for bringing a two inch long toy rifle to school.

That is sort of what happened in the instance cited by Luke above. Christ's adversaries are made to look foolish with their zero-tolerance of doing anything on the sabbath not on the list of approved activities. No one else was healing the sick, so the situation had not come up before. When confronted with something new like this healing people on the sabbath they fell back on the rules and were made to look foolish to the regular people who could see the illogic in forbidding a healing on the sabbath.

What Christ is doing is impressing people with the idea that these strict rules for the sabbath are wrong. It is a unique day. It should not be treated like just another day, but instead it should a day of worship. However, we should not allow rules that stand in the way of one person doing good for another just because that is not on the list of approved activities. In fact sabbath day rules should be loose enough to allow and even encourage doing helpful things on that day.

18 Then said he, Unto what is the kingdom of God like? and whereunto shall I resemble it?
19 It is like a grain of mustard seed, which a man took, and cast into his garden; and it grew, and waxed a great tree; and the fowls of the air lodged in the branches of it.
20 And again he said, Whereunto shall I liken the kingdom of God?
21 It is like leaven, which a woman took and hid in three measures of meal, till the whole was leavened.
22 And he went through the cities and villages, teaching, and journeying toward Jerusalem.
23 **Then said one unto him, Lord, are there few that be saved? And he said unto them,**
24 **Strive to enter in at the strait gate: for many, I say unto you, will seek to enter in, and shall not be able.**
25 **When once the master of the house is risen up, and hath shut to the door, and ye begin to stand without, and to knock at the door, saying, Lord, Lord, open unto us; and he shall answer and say unto you, I know you not whence ye are:**
26 **Then shall ye begin to say, We have eaten and drunk in thy presence, and thou hast taught in our streets.**
27 **But he shall say, I tell you, I know you not whence ye are; depart from me, all ye workers of iniquity.**

28 There shall be weeping and gnashing of teeth, when ye shall see
Abraham, and Isaac, and Jacob, and all the prophets, in the
kingdom of God, and you yourselves thrust out.

29 And they shall come from the east, and from the west, and from
the north, and from the south, and shall sit down in the kingdom of
God.

30 And, behold, there are last which shall be first, and there are
first which shall be last.

*I think that here we have a prophesy that more than just the
Children of Israel will be saved. He is envisioning the day when the
gospel is opened up to all God's children.*

*The Jews of Christ's day were very prejudiced against people
who were not Jewish. They looked down on others as being lesser
beings. They even treated the Samaritans (People who were half Jewish
and half gentile) like dirt. These feelings led them to revolt against
Roman rule twice and saw them slaughtered by the thousands, and
other thousands carried off into slavery.*

*Christ is saying to the Jews the day is coming when you will
have had your chance to get into the kingdom and the door will be
closed to you. Instead people will come from all over the world to sit
down in God's kingdom. He says that you, the first, who have had the
truth and gospel for ages will now be last for squandering your chance
and those who have been the last to hear the good news of the gospel
will be first in the kingdom. Your Jewishness will no longer grant you
favored status. Instead is will see you sent to the back of the line, so to
speak.*

31 The same day there came certain of the Pharisees, saying unto him,
Get thee out, and depart hence: for Herod will kill thee.

32 And he said unto them, Go ye, and tell that fox, Behold, I cast out devils, and I do cures today and tomorrow, and the third day I shall be perfected.

33 Nevertheless I must walk to day, and tomorrow, and the day following: for it cannot be that a prophet perish out of Jerusalem.

34 **O Jerusalem, Jerusalem, which killest the prophets, and stonest them that are sent unto thee; how often would I have gathered thy children together, as a hen doth gather her brood under her wings, and ye would not!**

35 **Behold, your house is left unto you desolate: and verily I say unto you, Ye shall not see me, until the time come when ye shall say, Blessed is he that cometh in the name of the Lord.**

What a magnificent Heavenly Father we have. His people, that kill the ones he sends to instruct them, that will kill his son. Those same people He still wants to gather under his wings and protect. That is the love of a parent. No stranger would show that kind of love and mercy. We need to cultivate that sort of love. It is the mark of our being one of Jesus disciples. He says that thereby will all men know we are his disciples, that we love one another. Not some catechism, not the apostle's creed, not some system of beliefs, and not our politics. They are all fine and dandy, but what marks us as his disciples is our love for each other, sometimes in spite of one of the above.

Chapter 14

1 And it came to pass, as he went into the house of one of the chief Pharisees to eat bread on the sabbath day, that they watched him.

2 And, behold, there was a certain man before him which had the dropsy.

3 And Jesus answering spake unto the lawyers and Pharisees, saying, Is it lawful to heal on the sabbath day?

4 And they held their peace. And he took him, and healed him, and let him go;

5 And answered them, saying, Which of you shall have an ass or an ox fallen into a pit, and will not straightway pull him out on the sabbath day?

6 And they could not answer him again to these things.

7 And he put forth a parable to those which were bidden, when he marked how they chose out the chief rooms; saying unto them,

8 When thou art bidden of any man to a wedding, sit not down in the highest room; lest a more honourable man than thou be bidden of him;

9 And he that bade thee and him come and say to thee, Give this man place; and thou begin with shame to take the lowest room.

10 But when thou art bidden, go and sit down in the lowest room; that when he that bade thee cometh, he may say unto thee, Friend, go up higher: then shalt thou have worship in the presence of them that sit at meat with thee.

11 **For whosoever exalteth himself shall be abased; and he that humbleth himself shall be exalted.**

So often men love to list their honors, their accomplishments. It

is reasonable. While others sat aside this man or woman entered the fray. Now they feel entitled to the honors they have earned. Our savior, however, says the opposite should be our practice. I think he is saying that when you pridefully exalt yourself, you have your reward in any adoration you receive. Whatever honor you deserve, you have it. I think it follows that in the next life, those who have earned honors but not but not taken them, will get what they have earned. Christ is saying that you can have honor here or there but not both. Honor in this life is transitory, but in the next it will abide. The choice is yours.

12 Then said he also to him that bade him, When thou makest a dinner or a supper, call not thy friends, nor thy brethren, neither thy kinsmen, nor thy rich neighbours; lest they also bid thee again, and a recompence be made thee.
13 But when thou makest a feast, call the poor, the maimed, the lame, the blind:
14 And thou shalt be blessed; for they cannot recompense thee: for thou shalt be recompensed at the resurrection of the just.

Here Christ is just reiterating what he said in verse 11. You can have your reward now or in God's kingdom, but you can't have both. I am afraid that most people, living as they do in the present will opt for the quick payoff. Taking the attitude of that old adage, that a bird in the hand is worth two in the bush. Christ, on the other hand, is counseling patience.

15 And when one of them that sat at meat with him heard these things, he said unto him, Blessed is he that shall eat bread in the kingdom of God.
16 Then said he unto him, A certain man made a great supper, and bade many:
17 And sent his servant at supper time to say to them that were bidden, Come; for all things are now ready.

18 And they all with one consent began to make excuse. The first said unto him, I have bought a piece of ground, and I must needs go and see it: I pray thee have me excused.

19 And another said, I have bought five yoke of oxen, and I go to prove them: I pray thee have me excused.

20 And another said, I have married a wife, and therefore I cannot come.

21 So that servant came, and shewed his lord these things. Then the master of the house being angry said to his servant, Go out quickly into the streets and lanes of the city, and bring in hither the poor, and the maimed, and the halt, and the blind.b

22 And the servant said, Lord, it is done as thou hast commanded, and yet there is room.

23 And the lord said unto the servant, Go out into the highways and hedges, and compel them to come in, that my house may be filled.

24 For I say unto you, That none of those men which were bidden shall taste of my supper.

25 And there went great multitudes with him: and he turned, and said unto them,

26 If any man come to me, and hate not his father, and mother, and wife, and children, and brethren, and sisters, yea, and his own life also, he cannot be my disciple.

27 And whosoever doth not bear his cross, and come after me, cannot be my disciple.

28 For which of you, intending to build a tower, sitteth not down first, and counteth the cost, whether he have sufficient to finish it?

29 Lest haply, after he hath laid the foundation, and is not able to finish it, all that behold it begin to mock him,

30 Saying, This man began to build, and was not able to finish.

31 Or what king, going to make war against another king, sitteth not down first, and consulteth whether he be able with ten thousand to meet him that cometh against him with twenty thousand?

32 Or else, while the other is yet a great way off, he sendeth an

ambassage, and desireth conditions of peace.

33 So likewise, whosoever he be of you that forsaketh not all that he hath, he cannot be my disciple.

It is not so much that every disciple gives up everything. However, we must consecrate all we have to Christ and his church. We must be ready to do that. Everything we own must be his for the asking. This is a commitment I have made. I enjoy my house, car, and other possessions, but will give them up if asked.

Brigham Young used to make announcements during church conferences that this family or that family were called to sell their homes and personal possessions and to move to some place else and start a town or do something that the church needed.

I live in Iron County, Utah. The name comes from the fact that Brigham did just as described above. The saints in Utah lived over a thousand miles from the nearest iron smelter. Any iron the church or church members needed had to be put in a wagon and hauled across the plains to Utah. However, the area where I live had limestone, coal, and iron ore, everything needed to produce Iron. Brigham, knowing the Church and its people needed iron, called a number of families to pull up stakes and move to this area and start mining and smelting iron. They did so. They felt that Brigham was telling them God's will for their lives and they obeyed. This is the sort of dedication Christ is speaking of.

34 Salt is good: but if the salt have lost his savour, wherewith shall it be seasoned?

35 It is neither fit for the land, nor yet for the dunghill; but men cast it out. He that hath ears to hear, let him hear.

Chapter 15

1 Then drew near unto him all the publicans and sinners for to hear him.

2 And the Pharisees and scribes murmured, saying, This man receiveth sinners, and eateth with them.

3 And he spake this parable unto them, saying,

4 What man of you, having an hundred sheep, if he lose one of them, doth not leave the ninety and nine in the wilderness, and go after that which is lost, until he find it?

5 And when he hath found it, he layeth it on his shoulders, rejoicing.

6 And when he cometh home, he calleth together his friends and neighbours, saying unto them, Rejoice with me; for I have found my sheep which was lost.

7 I say unto you, that likewise joy shall be in heaven over one sinner that repenteth, more than over ninety and nine just persons, which need no repentance.

I think Christ is playing on their vanity here. He is factiously saying you are the ninety-nine that don't need my help, so I will leave you behind while I search the wilderness for the sinners and eat with them while I look for my lost sheep. And in truth, He is willing to go among sinners to find his lost sheep. He will go whereever they are to find them. His church is made up of those who are and were in need of salvation. Finding the lost is what the church and Christ are all about. Christ's and the church's purpose is not to let us rest easy in Zion, but to challenge us to do more for others and the spreading of the gospel.

8 Either what woman having ten pieces of silver, if she lose one piece, doth not light a candle, and sweep the house, and seek diligently till she find it?

9 And when she hath found it, she calleth her friends and her neighbours together, saying, Rejoice with me; for I have found the piece which I had lost.

10 Likewise, I say unto you, there is joy in the presence of the angels of God over one sinner that repenteth.

11 And he said, A certain man had two sons:

12 And the younger of them said to his father, Father, give me the portion of goods that falleth to me. And he divided unto them his living.

13 And not many days after the younger son gathered all together, and took his journey into a far country, and there wasted his substance with riotous living.

14 And when he had spent all, there arose a mighty famine in that land; and he began to be in want.

15 And he went and joined himself to a citizen of that country; and he sent him into his fields to feed swine.

16 And he would fain have filled his belly with the husks that the swine did eat: and no man gave unto him.

17 And when he came to himself, he said, How many hired servants of my father's have bread enough and to spare, and I perish with hunger!

18 I will arise and go to my father, and will say unto him, Father, I have sinned against heaven, and before thee,

19 And am no more worthy to be called thy son: make me as one of thy hired servants.

20 And he arose, and came to his father. But when he was yet a great way off, his father saw him, and had compassion, and ran, and fell on his neck, and kissed him.

21 And the son said unto him, Father, I have sinned against heaven, and in thy sight, and am no more worthy to be called thy

son.

22 But the father said to his servants, Bring forth the best robe,
and put it on him; and put a ring on his hand, and shoes on his feet:

23 And bring hither the fatted calf, and kill it; and let us eat, and
be merry:

24 For this my son was dead, and is alive again; he was lost, and is
found. And they began to be merry.

25 Now his elder son was in the field: and as he came and drew
nigh to the house, he heard musick and dancing.

26 And he called one of the servants, and asked what these things
meant.

27 And he said unto him, Thy brother is come; and thy father hath
killed the fatted calf, because he hath received him safe and sound.

28 And he was angry, and would not go in: therefore came his
father out, and intreated him.

29 And he answering said to his father, Lo, these many years do I
serve thee, neither transgressed I at any time thy commandment:
and yet thou never gavest me a kid, that I might make merry with
my friends:

30 But as soon as this thy son was come, which hath devoured thy
living with harlots, thou hast killed for him the fatted calf.

31 And he said unto him, Son, thou art ever with me, and all that I
have is thine.

32 It was meet that we should make merry, and be glad: for this
thy brother was dead, and is alive again; and was lost, and is found.

*There are times when a big sinner finds his or her way to the
gospel. The missionaries penetrate their heart and the gospel flows in.
The sinful person is contrite and askes for baptism. How should we feel
towards that individual. This parable and the two previous all tell us
how Heavenly Father feels. He rejoices at the return of the lost sheep,
the misplaced coin, the prodigal son. Should we not do the same. Yet we
tend to be resentful if everyone is wooing and ahhing over the new*

convert while we who have been faithful all along get no special attention.

Chapter 16

1 And he said also unto his disciples, There was a certain rich man, which had a steward; and the same was accused unto him that he had wasted his goods.

2 And he called him, and said unto him, How is it that I hear this of thee? give an account of thy stewardship; for thou mayest be no longer steward.

3 Then the steward said within himself, What shall I do? for my lord taketh away from me the stewardship: I cannot dig; to beg I am ashamed.

4 I am resolved what to do, that, when I am put out of the stewardship, they may receive me into their houses.

5 So he called every one of his lord's debtors unto him, and said unto the first, How much owest thou unto my lord?

6 And he said, An hundred measures of oil. And he said unto him, Take thy bill, and sit down quickly, and write fifty.

7 Then said he to another, And how much owest thou? And he said, An hundred measures of wheat. And he said unto him, Take thy bill, and write fourscore.

8 And the lord commended the unjust steward, because he had done wisely: for the children of this world are in their generation wiser than the children of light.

9 And I say unto you, Make to yourselves friends of the mammon of unrighteousness; that, when ye fail, they may receive you into everlasting habitations.

10 He that is faithful in that which is least is faithful also in much: and he that is unjust in the least is unjust also in much.

11 If therefore ye have not been faithful in the unrighteous mammon, who will commit to your trust the true riches?

12 And if ye have not been faithful in that which is another man's, who shall give you that which is your own?

I can offer no light on that passage. Many of Christ's parables were offered as a way of hiding certain truths from the general public and revealing it only to His disciples. It is also a good rule not to base doctrine on parables. Christ's reason for telling them was not doctrinal but a source of practical lesions. What is to be learned here, I do not know.

13 No servant can serve two masters: for either he will hate the one, and love the other; or else he will hold to the one, and despise the other. Ye cannot serve God and mammon.

14 And the Pharisees also, who were covetous, heard all these things: and they derided him.

15 And he said unto them, Ye are they which justify yourselves before men; but God knoweth your hearts: for that which is highly esteemed among men is abomination in the sight of God.

16 The law and the prophets were until John: since that time the kingdom of God is preached, and every man presseth into it.

17 And it is easier for heaven and earth to pass, than one tittle of the law to fail.

18 Whosoever putteth away his wife, and marrieth another, committeth adultery: and whosoever marrieth her that is put away from her husband committeth adultery.

One of the things I most enjoy about my church is that it is subject to change. Admittedly, it can be slow in changing, and rightfully it clings to core principals that make it hard to be a good LDS member. Religion that is easy, however, does not serve a man or woman or child well. Religion needs to require effort. If it does not it will not be life changing, and then what good is it.

But back to the idea of change. If you accept the idea that when John finished the Book of Revelations that he put a period at the end of the last sentence and God's words to mankind were finished, well, that is your right. However, I do not believe God quit revealing things to His children or that his law was settled forever. Society has changed and the church along with it. The church has changed because it has a prophet and a form of governance or polity that allows for continued revelations. So, in cases like the above where Christ speaks as he does on adultery, it may not be the final word. People, the church, and church members can change and what was not allowed can now be allowed without sin.

This is one reason we should not be overly dogmatic on one hand or too free in what we toss out of the law on the other. One of the biggest problems Christ had was Sabbath keeping, or at least Sabbath keeping as it was taught in His day by the Scribes and Pharisees.

Now a strict following of the Law of Moses would require the stoning to death of people who work on the Sabbath.

A strict following of the Mosaic Law would have us buying and selling slaves, killing farmers that planted beans next to corn, not eating pork, killing homosexuals, etc. But we don't do those things. I do not know of a church that calls for adherence to those laws. They are largely ignored today,

Another sin that has lost its sinfulness is remarrying. Effort should be made to protect marriages. Divorce should be a last resort. However, it should be on the table and an option when a wife and husband no longer have a good marriage and the chances of it ever being good again are slim to none.

I tried to keep my first marriage together much longer than I should have and as a result went through a lot of mental pain and agony when I could have been seeking the solace of another. At least it convinced me of the solemnity of the marriage vow and a determination to never be the one who breaks it should I marry again. Not only is it a covenant between and man and a woman, it is a covenant between them both and God.

19 There was a certain rich man, which was clothed in purple and fine linen, and fared sumptuously every day:

20 And there was a certain beggar named Lazarus, which was laid at his gate, full of sores,

21 And desiring to be fed with the crumbs which fell from the rich man's table: moreover the dogs came and licked his sores.

22 And it came to pass, that the beggar died, and was carried by the angels into Abraham's bosom: the rich man also died, and was buried;

23 And in hell he lift up his eyes, being in torments, and seeth Abraham afar off, and Lazarus in his bosom.

24 And he cried and said, Father Abraham, have mercy on me, and send Lazarus, that he may dip the tip of his finger in water, and cool my tongue; for I am tormented in this flame.

25 But Abraham said, Son, remember that thou in thy lifetime receivedst thy good things, and likewise Lazarus evil things: but now he is comforted, and thou art tormented.

26 **And beside all this, between us and you there is a great gulf fixed: so that they which would pass from hence to you cannot; neither can they pass to us, that would come from thence.**

This is a well told parable. Most have heard it many times. As I pointed out above, it is also a good rule not to base doctrine on parables. Christ's reason for telling them was not doctrinal but a source of practical lesions. Having said that, it is interesting to note the

picture Christ paints of a separation between the good and the bad in the afterlife, a separation that allows no physical crossing between but allows sight and communication between to two. I wonder if that part is true?

Also, the scene of the rich man in hell. It was for sure to rouse no protests among His listeners. It fit the popular view of the afterlife awaiting the wicked. Maybe Christ used it for that reason. However, I do not believe that a loving God is going to toss a third of his children into a lake of fire and leave them there to writhe in pain for eternity.

27 Then he said, I pray thee therefore, father, that thou wouldest send him to my father's house:
28 For I have five brethren; that he may testify unto them, lest they also come into this place of torment.
29 Abraham saith unto him, They have Moses and the prophets; let them hear them.
30 And he said, Nay, father Abraham: but if one went unto them from the dead, they will repent.
31 And he said unto him, If they hear not Moses and the prophets, neither will they be persuaded, though one rose from the dead.

Chapter 17

1 Then said he unto the disciples, It is impossible but that offences will come: but woe unto him, through whom they come!
2 **It were better for him that a millstone were hanged about his neck, and he cast into the sea, than that he should offend one of these little ones.**

Children have an innate simple faith. They trust their parents and what their parents teach them. Skepticism comes later along with growth and years. Yet a foundation of faith can be laid in a child's early years. Christ is telling us that those that destroy that child's faith are in big trouble.

3 Take heed to yourselves: If thy brother trespass against thee, rebuke him; and if he repent, forgive him.
4 And if he trespass against thee seven times in a day, and seven times in a day turn again to thee, saying, I repent; thou shalt forgive him.
5 And the apostles said unto the Lord, Increase our faith.
6 And the Lord said, If ye had faith as a grain of mustard seed, ye might say unto this sycamine tree, Be thou plucked up by the root, and be thou planted in the sea; and it should obey you.
7 But which of you, having a servant plowing or feeding cattle, will say unto him by and by, when he is come from the field, Go and sit down to meat?
8 And will not rather say unto him, Make ready wherewith I may sup, and gird thyself, and serve me, till I have eaten and drunken; and afterward thou shalt eat and drink?
9 Doth he thank that servant because he did the things that were

commanded him? I know not.

10 So likewise ye, when ye shall have done all those things which are commanded you, say, We are unprofitable servants: we have done that which was our duty to do.

God expects us to go the 2nd mile. It is not enough to do what is expected of us. That is something less than the minimum. That is the floor of our service. We must excel at doing good. Compassionate service is expected of us. Taking care of each other. We should have our eyes open and be looking for opportunities to do good works. This is what I wrote of above. Religion that does not challenge us and make it hard for us is a religion of little or no value. A religion that consists of subscribing to a set of beliefs is unprofitable, at best. If it is not life changing it is nothing.

So many people have the God gene. They do not have to be taught to believe in God. It comes natural to them. However, what they do with that natural proclivity towards religiosity varies from person to person. Many are content to follow a set of rules they think will make God happy. Others perform rites and rituals that they hope will please God. They all miss the mark. What our Heavenly Father wants of us is for us to live lives like that pictured for us in the Gospel of Luke. He wants us to take our lead from the savior and follow in His footsteps. As he told the rich young ruler, "Come follow me." He wants us to pattern our lives after his. He wants us to live lives of love and service.

11 And it came to pass, as he went to Jerusalem, that he passed through the midst of Samaria and Galilee.

12 And as he entered into a certain village, there met him ten men that were lepers, which stood afar off:

13 And they lifted up their voices, and said, Jesus, Master, have mercy on us.

14 And when he saw them, he said unto them, Go shew yourselves

unto the priests. And it came to pass, that, as they went, they were cleansed.

15 And one of them, when he saw that he was healed, turned back, and with a loud voice glorified God,

16 And fell down on his face at his feet, giving him thanks: and he was a Samaritan.

The Jews of Jesus time were extremely prejudiced. Knowing themselves to be God's chosen people, they looked down on everybody else. They were expecting a Messiah to come and lead them in kicking the Romans out of their country and making them the number one people in the world, to bring back the glory days of King David.

They disliked everyone else, but they had a particular dislike of Samaritans who lived right in the middle of what is today called the Holy Land. There were Jews to the north and south with them right in the center. These were people who were part Jew and part Gentile, Hybrids. A mixing of people and blood and religion. They were looked down on much as a person of mixed white and black ancestry would have been looked down on in the Jim Crow South of a hundred or hundred and twenty years ago.

The Samaritans worshiped God but did not go to the Temple in Jerusalem. They were not welcomed there. Instead they had their own temple of sorts. They avoided Jews and Jews avoided them. But not Jesus. Where normally a Jew going from Galilee to Jerusalem would go around Samaria to avoid having to see or deal with Samaritans, Jesus cuts right through their country. What a lesson for those who claim to be Christian yet are bigoted against other people, be they refugees, another race, or just from another part of the country.

As He is passing through, he meets these ten lepers. Lepers were allowed no contact with people that did not have the disease. They had

no idea of germs in those days, but they knew that if you were in contact with a leper you stood a good chance of getting the disease yourself. That is why they stood at a distance while asking for mercy (healing) from Jesus.

Jesus obliges them, but when they see that the disease is gone only one of the ten returns to say thank you. Sad but typical. I can just hear all the promises they were making to God before they met with Jesus. Oh, if they were just healed they'd do this and that. However, when they are healed the promises are soon forgotten. They say there are no atheists in a fox hole. But when the battle moves on and they have been spared they forget all the prayers and begging that went on while shells were exploding and bullets whizzing by.

Also of note is Jesus telling them to go and show themselves to a priest. If you had a disease that made you "Unclean" like leprosy, and you thought you were healed, you would go to a priest and he would look you over and decide if you were really healed or not. Only after the priest pronounced you clean could you go back and live with your family or others that did not have the disease.

Now here is Jesus telling a Samaritan to go present himself to a priest. But wait, Samaritans had a religion of their own, and were not considered part of the Jewish sect. Their priests taught a form of the Jewish religion but not exactly the same. They worshiped God, but not the same way as the Jews. They had their own temple. They had some of what the Jews would call heathen practices. Their priests would be thought of as some sort of apostates, and here Jesus is telling the healed leper to go to those priests so they could declare them clean.

Jesus sending the former leper to such a man says to me that a Samaritan priest could be a good man and serve God in the best way he knew, and God would honor his faithfulness. What God expects of us is that we are true and faithful to the knowledge given us. I mentioned before how Paul found some disciples of John the Baptist living in what is today Turkey (They had probably fled there when John was killed). Paul taught them the whole gospel, they accepted it and where given the Gift of the Holy Spirit. They were living up to the knowledge given them and God honored that by sending Paul to them.

Once again, I think we can see here that more important than doctrinal purity is, are we feeding God's sheep. That is what our Father in Heaven wants of us. As far as we know, that was Christ's final command to Peter, "Feed my sheep." That was a command given to Peter, but meant for all of us.

17 And Jesus answering said, Were there not ten cleansed? but where are the nine?
18 There are not found that returned to give glory to God, save this stranger.
19 And he said unto him, Arise, go thy way: thy faith hath made thee whole.
20 **And when he was demanded of the Pharisees, when the kingdom of God should come, he answered them and said, The kingdom of God cometh not with observation:**
21 **Neither shall they say, Lo here! or, lo there! for, behold, the kingdom of God is within you.**

This is more of the Jews idea of a Messiah that will lead them in throwing out the Romans and establishing a Jewish kingdom. But Jesus says, "No, it isn't a physical kingdom, it is a spiritual one.

22 And he said unto the disciples, The days will come, when ye shall desire to see one of the days of the Son of man, and ye shall not see it.
23 And they shall say to you, See here; or, see there: go not after them, nor follow them.

24 For as the lightning, that lighteneth out of the one part under heaven, shineth unto the other part under heaven; so shall also the Son of man be in his day.

25 But first must he suffer many things, and be rejected of this generation.

26 And as it was in the days of Noe, so shall it be also in the days of the Son of man.

27 They did eat, they drank, they married wives, they were given in marriage, until the day that Noe entered into the ark, and the flood came, and destroyed them all.

28 Likewise also as it was in the days of Lot; they did eat, they drank, they bought, they sold, they planted, they builded;

29 But the same day that Lot went out of Sodom it rained fire and brimstone from heaven, and destroyed them all.

30 Even thus shall it be in the day when the Son of man is revealed.

31 In that day, he which shall be upon the housetop, and his stuff in the house, let him not come down to take it away: and he that is in the field, let him likewise not return back.

32 Remember Lot's wife.

33 **Whosoever shall seek to save his life shall lose it; and whosoever shall lose his life shall preserve it.**

34 **I tell you, in that night there shall be two men in one bed; the one shall be taken, and the other shall be left.**

35 **Two women shall be grinding together; the one shall be taken, and the other left.**

36 **Two men shall be in the field; the one shall be taken, and the other left.**

37 **And they answered and said unto him, Where, Lord? And he said unto them, Wheresoever the body is, thither will the eagles be gathered together.**

Jesus is speaking of the "Rapture," when he will come to earth again, this time to rule. As a prelude those who have followed him, but died before he comes will be raised from the dead and caught up to meet him in the sky. At that same time faithful followers who are living at the time of his coming will be caught up too, in order to meet him in the sky. It is those people that the verses above speak of. People just going about their jobs and lives and the faithful will be called out and the others left. A wonderful day for Jesus followers, a sad day for those left behind.

Chapter 18

1 And he spake a parable unto them to this end, that men ought always to pray, and not to faint;

2 Saying, There was in a city a judge, which feared not God, neither regarded man:

3 And there was a widow in that city; and she came unto him, saying, Avenge me of mine adversary.

4 And he would not for a while: but afterward he said within himself, Though I fear not God, nor regard man;

5 Yet because this widow troubleth me, I will avenge her, lest by her continual coming she weary me.

6 And the Lord said, Hear what the unjust judge saith.

7 And shall not God avenge his own elect, which cry day and night unto him, though he bear long with them?

8 I tell you that he will avenge them speedily. Nevertheless when the Son of man cometh, shall he find faith on the earth?

9 **And he spake this parable unto certain which trusted in themselves that they were righteous, and despised others:**

10 **Two men went up into the temple to pray; the one a Pharisee, and the other a publican.**

11 **The Pharisee stood and prayed thus with himself, God, I thank thee, that I am not as other men are, extortioners, unjust, adulterers, or even as this publican.**

12 **I fast twice in the week, I give tithes of all that I possess.**

13 **And the publican, standing afar off, would not lift up so much as his eyes unto heaven, but smote upon his breast, saying, God be merciful to me a sinner.**

14 **I tell you, this man went down to his house justified rather than the other: for every one that exalteth himself shall be abased; and**

he that humbleth himself shall be exalted.

One of Satan's favorite ways drawing us into sin is to get us to compare ourselves with others. He gets us to develop this "Holier than Thou" attitude when we deal with family, friends, or just the people we meet with every day. He gets a man or woman to start looking down on others. It then becomes easier to excuse a failing here or there because, after all I do do this and that so much better than other people. Depending on how much better we see ourselves as compared to our neighbors, just that much we allow ourselves to sin and believe we are okay.

15 And they brought unto him also infants, that he would touch them: but when his disciples saw it, they rebuked them.
16 But Jesus called them unto him, and said, Suffer little children to come unto me, and forbid them not: for of such is the kingdom of God.
17 Verily I say unto you, Whosoever shall not receive the kingdom of God as a little child shall in no wise enter therein.

A child can trust in ways we, as adults find difficult. I am picturing in my mind a child that, let's say, climbs up on a countertop or table. Then that child yells, "Daddy catch me," and launches themselves off the table and into the air in complete confidence that daddy is going to catch them and not allow them to be hurt. It is hard for an adult, with all our doubts and fears, to do something like that. However, that is the sort of faith Christ is looking for in us. He wants us to shout "Catch me," and then leap for his arms in complete confidence that he will catch us.

18 And a certain ruler asked him, saying, Good Master, what shall I do to inherit eternal life?

19 And Jesus said unto him, Why callest thou me good? none is good, save one, that is, God.

20 Thou knowest the commandments, Do not commit adultery, Do not kill, Do not steal, Do not bear false witness, Honour thy father and thy mother.

21 And he said, All these have I kept from my youth up.

22 Now when Jesus heard these things, he said unto him, Yet lackest thou one thing: sell all that thou hast, and distribute unto the poor, and thou shalt have treasure in heaven: and come, follow me.

23 And when he heard this, he was very sorrowful: for he was very rich.

24 And when Jesus saw that he was very sorrowful, he said, How hardly shall they that have riches enter into the kingdom of God!

25 For it is easier for a camel to go through a needle's eye, than for a rich man to enter into the kingdom of God.

26 And they that heard it said, Who then can be saved?

27 And he said, The things which are impossible with men are possible with God.

There is something about possessions that we just want to hold on to them. In most cases we have worked for and earned them through our labor, either physical or mental. Now that we have them we rarely want to share. That is the place this young man finds himself in. He has lived a good life and life has been good. However, he wants to make sure he does well in the next life too. But Christ tells him to give up those things that make this life so good in order to ready himself for the next life. That is too hard to do, and he goes away sad. When the disciples see all this they say "Who, then, can get into heaven." Christ answers that it is easier for a camel to go through the eye of a needle that for a rich man to get into God's heavenly kingdom.

There are two lessons to learn here.

1st, it is a common saying that, "You can't take it with you," referring to taking this life's possessions into the next, and it is true. You can't. However, you can send it on ahead. Doing good deeds in this life is like putting deposits in your heavenly bank account. God watches how we treat others and rewards us accordingly in the next life.

2nd, Christ did not completely close the door on people of wealth. As I have mentioned before, he said, it is easier for a camel to pass through a needle's eye that for a rich person to go to heaven. He did not say it was impossible. For us living today, it may seem like he is closing the door pretty tight on rich folk with that camel and needle thing, but if you lived in Christ's time you would see that while difficult for the well to do, heaven is still open to them. You see, in those days most cities were walled and had big huge gates that they could close at night and keep the unwanted (read armies of the enemy) out. During the day the city gate would be open and people passing in and out while lookouts and soldiers watched for trouble. If they saw an enemy force coming they could shut the gate and the city would be safe.

At night, however, it was dark so the gates were always shut. If a force snuck up on the city under the cover of night, they would not be able to get in. But, life being what it is some good innocent people would not be able to to arrive at the city before dark, and would find themselves locked out. To deal with such a contingency, a small almost man-sized door would be put into the city wall. It was designed small so only one person at a time could get through. The city's defenders could keep out unwanted or enemies if they could only get in one at a time. For obvious reasons, this small entrance into the city was called "the eye of the needle."

Occasionally a late arrival to the city would be riding a camel. He would want to bring it into the city too. By unloading the camel of

*the saddle and anything else it was carrying, and getting it to kneel
down lower it head, and inch forward on its knees the camel could
squeeze through the opening, not an easy thing to do, but possible.
Camels did not like this process and would bite and spit and generally
resist. It was a lot of work, but it could be done. The same is true of the
rich man getting into heaven.*

28 Then Peter said, Lo, we have left all, and followed thee.
29 And he said unto them, Verily I say unto you, There is no man that
hath left house, or parents, or brethren, or wife, or children, for the
kingdom of God's sake,
30 Who shall not receive manifold more in this present time, and in
the world to come life everlasting.
31 **Then he took unto him the twelve, and said unto them, Behold,
we go up to Jerusalem, and all things that are written by the
prophets concerning the Son of man shall be accomplished.**
32 **For he shall be delivered unto the Gentiles, and shall be
mocked, and spitefully entreated, and spitted on:**
33 **And they shall scourge him, and put him to death: and the
third day he shall rise again.**
34 **And they understood none of these things: and this saying was
hid from them, neither knew they the things which were spoken.**

*As I am writing this book I often find myself thinking that the
twelve disciples were some of the dumbest people around. Christ would
tell them things again and again and they still would not believe what
He said, or they might believe, but what they believed was wrong. These
are men who would rock the world one day when they went out
preaching after Christ's death, resurrection, and His return to heaven.
Yet here they are acting just plain dumb. How is the transition made,
how do they go from this stage to being mighty men of God? I think the
answer is the Holy Spirit. They will be filled with power at the feast of*

Pentecost after Christ has left them and returned to Heavenly Father. We each need our own Pentecost. We need the filling of the Holy Spirit. In that filling is faith and power.

35 And it came to pass, that as he was come nigh unto Jericho, a certain blind man sat by the way side begging:

36 And hearing the multitude pass by, he asked what it meant.

37 And they told him, that Jesus of Nazareth passeth by.

38 And he cried, saying, Jesus, thou Son of David, have mercy on me.

39 And they which went before rebuked him, that he should hold his peace: but he cried so much the more, Thou Son of David, have mercy on me.

40 And Jesus stood, and commanded him to be brought unto him: and when he was come near, he asked him,

41 Saying, What wilt thou that I shall do unto thee? And he said, Lord, that I may receive my sight.

42 And Jesus said unto him, Receive thy sight: thy faith hath saved thee.

43 And immediately he received his sight, and followed him, glorifying God: and all the people, when they saw it, gave praise unto God.

Another healing, another blind man receives his sight. Our master was so compassionate. Others are telling the blind man to shut up. The blind man just yells louder. Christ hears and heals him. Why? Because he cares. I can think of no place in the New Testament record that Christ turns away a person needing and asking for healing. How do we react to those needing our help in this world. Do we reject them? Do we look down on them. Or do we reach out a helping hand. I am moved to tears by the words of a poem inscribed on a plaque in front of the Statue of Liberty:

It is because we as a nation took those words to heart that today this is the greatest country in the world. We must never let our leaders or the haters that follow them to put that lamp out.

Chapter 19

1 And Jesus entered and passed through Jericho.

2 And, behold, there was a man named Zacchaeus, which was the chief among the publicans, and he was rich.

3 And he sought to see Jesus who he was; and could not for the press, because he was little of stature.

4 And he ran before, and climbed up into a sycamore tree to see him: for he was to pass that way.

5 And when Jesus came to the place, he looked up, and saw him, and said unto him, Zacchaeus, make haste, and come down; for today I must abide at thy house.

6 And he made haste, and came down, and received him joyfully.

7 And when they saw it, they all murmured, saying, That he was gone to be guest with a man that is a sinner.

8 And Zacchaeus stood, and said unto the Lord; Behold, Lord, the half of my goods I give to the poor; and if I have taken anything from any man by false accusation, I restore him fourfold.

9 And Jesus said unto him, This day is salvation come to this house, forsomuch as he also is a son of Abraham.

10 For the Son of man is come to seek and to save that which was lost.

We all start out lost. I am not speaking of the idea of original sin, that we are tainted by our decent from Adam. We are lost because we have forgotten our preexistence. Christ, however, came to find us, to seek us out and save our blind selves and prepare us for a future with Him in the kingdom of God.

Zacchaeus words to Christ read in the past tense. However, I think he is saying that these are things he is going to do. I say this because Christ says "This day is salvation come to this house."

11 And as they heard these things, he added and spake a parable, because he was nigh to Jerusalem, and because they thought that the kingdom of God should immediately appear.

Parables are difficult to understand and because they are deliberately obscure you can never be sure you have the right meaning or are interpreting them correctly. For those reasons I pretty much stay away from parables and leave their explanation to those wiser than I.

12 He said therefore, A certain nobleman went into a far country to receive for himself a kingdom, and to return.
13 And he called his ten servants, and delivered them ten pounds, and said unto them, Occupy till I come.
14 But his citizens hated him, and sent a message after him, saying, We will not have this man to reign over us.
15 And it came to pass, that when he was returned, having received the kingdom, then he commanded these servants to be called unto him, to whom he had given the money, that he might know how much every man had gained by trading.
16 Then came the first, saying, Lord, thy pound hath gained ten pounds.
17 And he said unto him, Well, thou good servant: because thou hast been faithful in a very little, have thou authority over ten cities.
18 And the second came, saying, Lord, thy pound hath gained five pounds.
19 And he said likewise to him, Be thou also over five cities.
20 And another came, saying, Lord, behold, here is thy pound, which I have kept laid up in a napkin:
21 For I feared thee, because thou art an austere man: thou takest up that thou layedst not down, and reapest that thou didst not sow.

22 And he saith unto him, Out of thine own mouth will I judge thee, thou wicked servant. Thou knewest that I was an austere man, taking up that I laid not down, and reaping that I did not sow:

23 Wherefore then gavest not thou my money into the bank, that at my coming I might have required mine own with usury?

24 And he said unto them that stood by, Take from him the pound, and give it to him that hath ten pounds.

25 (And they said unto him, Lord, he hath ten pounds.)

26 For I say unto you, That unto every one which hath shall be given; and from him that hath not, even that he hath shall be taken away from him.

27 But those mine enemies, which would not that I should reign over them, bring hither, and slay them before me.

28 And when he had thus spoken, he went before, ascending up to Jerusalem.

29 And it came to pass, when he was come nigh to Bethphage and Bethany, at the mount called the mount of Olives, he sent two of his disciples,

30 Saying, Go ye into the village over against you; in the which at your entering ye shall find a colt tied, whereon yet never man sat: loose him, and bring him hither.

31 And if any man ask you, Why do ye loose him? thus shall ye say unto him, Because the Lord hath need of him.

32 And they that were sent went their way, and found even as he had said unto them.

33 And as they were loosing the colt, the owners thereof said unto them, Why loose ye the colt?

34 And they said, The Lord hath need of him.

35 And they brought him to Jesus: and they cast their garments upon the colt, and they set Jesus thereon.

36 And as he went, they spread their clothes in the way.

37 And when he was come nigh, even now at the descent of the mount of Olives, the whole multitude of the disciples began to

**rejoice and praise God with a loud voice for all the mighty works
that they had seen;**

*This must have been quite a sight, Christ riding in triumph into
Jerusalem. The Messiah, the Son of God arriving in the City of David.
Most, if not all, believing He is come to throw out the Romans and set
up a Jewish kingdom. Little do they understand (even thought Jesus had
told the time and again) he was going to Jerusalem to die, not become
king. He was going to the cross, he was going to pay the price of our
sins. He was going to make our salvation possible.*

38 Saying, Blessed be the King that cometh in the name of the Lord:
peace in heaven, and glory in the highest.
39 And some of the Pharisees from among the multitude said unto
him, Master, rebuke thy disciples.
40 And he answered and said unto them, I tell you that, if these should
hold their peace, the stones would immediately cry out.
41 **And when he was come near, he beheld the city, and wept over
it,**

*It is hard to put yourself in Christ's position and have the same
feelings He had. Even though he knows these people will turn on him
and kill him before the week is out, He still weeps over and for them.
These are the actions of wonderful, spiritual, loving, and the adjectives
go on, person. One who is worthy of our worship and one we should be
only too happy to follow.*

42 Saying, If thou hadst known, even thou, at least in this thy day, the
things which belong unto thy peace! but now they are hid from thine
eyes.
43 For the days shall come upon thee, that thine enemies shall cast a
trench about thee, and compass thee round, and keep thee in on every

side,

44 And shall lay thee even with the ground, and thy children within thee; and they shall not leave in thee one stone upon another; because thou knewest not the time of thy visitation.

45 **And he went into the temple, and began to cast out them that sold therein, and them that bought;**

The Jewish people thought of the temple as a very sacred place that should not be contaminated by non-Jewish items. This included money. So, if you came a long way and wanted to have an animal sacrificed for your sins, very often you would not have the animal with you, and you would need to buy one when you got there. However, the priests did not want you bringing tainted Roman money into the temple. So, money changers set up tables where you could turn in your Roman money for temple money. Christ did not object to this, but he hated that these money changers insisted on making large profits on the exchange. A temple dollar (if they used dollars which I doubt) might cost a pilgrim a dollar twenty. This turning a profit on other people's attempts to find forgiveness and salvation truly angered the Lord and He turned their tables over and drove them out with a whip.

46 Saying unto them, It is written, My house is the house of prayer: but ye have made it a den of thieves.

47 And he taught daily in the temple. But the chief priests and the scribes and the chief of the people sought to destroy him,

48 And could not find what they might do: for all the people were very attentive to hear him.

Chapter 20

1 And it came to pass, that on one of those days, as he taught the people in the temple, and preached the gospel, the chief priests and the scribes came upon him with the elders,

2 And spake unto him, saying, Tell us, by what authority doest thou these things? or who is he that gave thee this authority?

3 And he answered and said unto them, I will also ask you one thing; and answer me:

4 The baptism of John, was it from heaven, or of men?

5 And they reasoned with themselves, saying, If we shall say, From heaven; he will say, Why then believed ye him not?

6 But and if we say, Of men; all the people will stone us: for they be persuaded that John was a prophet.

7 And they answered, that they could not tell whence it was.

8 And Jesus said unto them, Neither tell I you by what authority I do these things.

9 Then began he to speak to the people this parable; A certain man planted a vineyard, and let it forth to husbandmen, and went into a far country for a long time.

10 And at the season he sent a servant to the husbandmen, that they should give him of the fruit of the vineyard: but the husbandmen beat him, and sent him away empty.

11 And again he sent another servant: and they beat him also, and entreated him shamefully, and sent him away empty.

12 And again he sent a third: and they wounded him also, and cast him out.

13 Then said the lord of the vineyard, What shall I do? I will send my beloved son: it may be they will reverence him when they see

him.

14 But when the husbandmen saw him, they reasoned among themselves, saying, This is the heir: come, let us kill him, that the inheritance may be ours.

15 So they cast him out of the vineyard, and killed him. **What therefore shall the lord of the vineyard do unto them?**

16 **He shall come and destroy these husbandmen, and shall give the vineyard to others. And when they heard it, they said, God forbid.**

This is a foretelling of taking of the gospel to the Gentiles and the person who would do that was Paul. I wonder if Paul might have been in the group that was sent to try to confound Christ. Of course we have no way of knowing, but it would not surprise me to find out he was there. He would be at the stoning of Stephen which took place only a few months after this incident.

17 And he beheld them, and said, What is this then that is written, The stone which the builders rejected, the same is become the head of the corner?

18 Whosoever shall fall upon that stone shall be broken; but on whomsoever it shall fall, it will grind him to powder.

19 And the chief priests and the scribes the same hour sought to lay hands on him; and they feared the people: for they perceived that he had spoken this parable against them.

20 And they watched him, and sent forth spies, which should feign themselves just men, that they might take hold of his words, that so they might deliver him unto the power and authority of the governor.

21 And they asked him, saying, Master, we know that thou sayest and teachest rightly, neither acceptest thou the person of any, but teachest the way of God truly:

22 Is it lawful for us to give tribute unto Caesar, or no?

23 But he perceived their craftiness, and said unto them, Why tempt ye me?

24 Shew me a penny. Whose image and superscription hath it? They answered and said, Caesar's.

25 And he said unto them, Render therefore unto Caesar the things which be Caesar's, and unto God the things which be God's.

26 And they could not take hold of his words before the people: and they marvelled at his answer, and held their peace.

27 Then came to him certain of the Sadducees, which deny that there is any resurrection; and they asked him,

28 Saying, Master, Moses wrote unto us, If any man's brother die, having a wife, and he die without children, that his brother should take his wife, and raise up seed unto his brother.

29 There were therefore seven brethren: and the first took a wife, and died without children.

30 And the second took her to wife, and he died childless.

31 And the third took her; and in like manner the seven also: and they left no children, and died.

32 Last of all the woman died also.

33 Therefore in the resurrection whose wife of them is she? for seven had her to wife.

34 And Jesus answering said unto them, The children of this world marry, and are given in marriage:

35 But they which shall be accounted worthy to obtain that world, and the resurrection from the dead, neither marry, nor are given in marriage:

36 Neither can they die any more: for they are equal unto the angels; and are the children of God, being the children of the resurrection.

37 Now that the dead are raised, even Moses shewed at the bush, when he calleth the Lord the God of Abraham, and the God of Isaac, and the God of Jacob.

38 For he is not a God of the dead, but of the living: for all live

unto him.

39 Then certain of the scribes answering said, Master, thou hast well said.
40 And after that they durst not ask him any question at all.
41 And he said unto them, How say they that Christ is David's son?
42 And David himself saith in the book of Psalms, The LORD said unto my Lord, Sit thou on my right hand,
43 Till I make thine enemies thy footstool.
44 David therefore calleth him Lord, how is he then his son?
45 Then in the audience of all the people he said unto his disciples,
46 Beware of the scribes, which desire to walk in long robes, and love greetings in the markets, and the highest seats in the synagogues, and the chief rooms at feasts;
47 Which devour widows' houses, and for a shew make long prayers: the same shall receive greater damnation.

Chapter 21

1 And he looked up, and saw the rich men casting their gifts into the treasury.

2 And he saw also a certain poor widow casting in thither two mites.

3 And he said, Of a truth I say unto you, that this poor widow hath cast in more than they all:

4 For all these have of their abundance cast in unto the offerings of God: but she of her penury hath cast in all the living that she had.

It is comforting to know that Heavenly Father does not look on the amount of money we give to His work, but rather he looks on the sacrifice we make to give to His Kingdom. A tithe (10%) is the least of what is expected. However it is a floor and not a ceiling. I for one can attest that I derive greater joy from the few dollars I can give over and above my tithe, than the tithe itself even though that 10% is the lion share of my giving.

Still I am moved by this poor woman who will, I surmise, miss a meal or two because of that giving. Give till it hurts, or your stomach, at least, hurts. That is her lesson for us.

Also, on the subject of giving, I am careful of the charities I give to. When I read of the huge salaries that the heads of various charities award themselves I grow sick. In fact, I give to none of them except the Salvation Army and my church. My church because I know the money will be well spent, and the Salvation Army for the same reason.

5 And as some spake of the temple, how it was adorned with goodly stones and gifts, he said,
6 As for these things which ye behold, the days will come, in the which there shall not be left one stone upon another, that shall not be thrown down.

This prophecy came true about forty years after Christ's crucifixion when the Romans burnt the temple as well as most of Jerusalem to the ground. As the verse above indicates the temple was richly adorned, with lots of gold on the walls and furnishings. When the building was burnt this gold melted and the liquid gold seeped between the stones. When the fire was over and the place cooled down the Roman soldiers pried the stones apart to get to the gold. They destroyed everything in their hunt for the gold. Thus Christ's prophecy was literally fulfilled. No stone was left unturned.

7 And they asked him, saying, Master, but when shall these things be? and what sign will there be when these things shall come to pass?
8 And he said, Take heed that ye be not deceived: for many shall come in my name, saying, I am Christ; and the time draweth near: go ye not therefore after them.

God says no one is to know, and none will be able to put a date to it. Then He warns us not to follow those who claim to know, yet how many have bene carried off by these false prophets. Those that claim to know the time of the Lord's return almost always lead others into sin or foolishness. Men have looked around and thought the time was close. Even the apostle Paul expected it to happen in his lifetime. He did not try to set a date, but a careful reading of his writings reveals that he lived his life expecting the Lord to come back soon, yet almost two thousand years have transpired since Paul's time and Christ still tarries.

Living a good life so that you have nothing to be ashamed of if Christ does come is a noble and righteous thing. However, being profligate in spending or lifestyle, and taking a "eat, drink, and be merry, for tomorrow we die" attitude is foolish. It was not too many years ago our country had a Secretary of the Interior who thought that Christ was coming soon and so it did not matter how the environment was trashed by mining, energy creation, deforestation, etc. He said Christ is coming soon so it did not matter how we treated our planet. Many projects were approved that should not have been. The man was a fool and we are paying the price for his foolishness today.

9 But when ye shall hear of wars and commotions, be not terrified: for these things must first come to pass; but the end is not by and by.
10 Then said he unto them, Nation shall rise against nation, and kingdom against kingdom:
11 And great earthquakes shall be in divers places, and famines, and pestilences; and fearful sights and great signs shall there be from heaven.

The above verses speak of what is almost the norm for humanity. Any of those things innumerated above could be in tomorrow's headlines and it would be no surprise.

12 But before all these, they shall lay their hands on you, and persecute you, delivering you up to the synagogues, and into prisons, being brought before kings and rulers for my name's sake.

Luke, the author of this Gospel, traveled with the Apostle Paul on portions of this missionary journeys. He knew Paul. This verse is an

13 And it shall turn to you for a testimony.

14 Settle it therefore in your hearts, not to meditate before what ye
shall answer:

15 For I will give you a mouth and wisdom, which all your
adversaries shall not be able to gainsay nor resist.

16 And ye shall be betrayed both by parents, and brethren, and
kinsfolks, and friends; and some of you shall they cause to be put to
death.

17 And ye shall be hated of all men for my name's sake.

18 But there shall not an hair of your head perish.

19 In your patience possess ye your souls.

20 And when ye shall see Jerusalem compassed with armies, then
know that the desolation thereof is nigh.

21 Then let them which are in Judaea flee to the mountains; and
let them which are in the midst of it depart out; and let not them
that are in the countries enter thereinto.

22 For these be the days of vengeance, that all things which are
written may be fulfilled.

23 But woe unto them that are with child, and to them that give
suck, in those days! for there shall be great distress in the land, and
wrath upon this people.

24 And they shall fall by the edge of the sword, and shall be led
away captive into all nations: and Jerusalem shall be trodden down
of the Gentiles, until the times of the Gentiles be fulfilled.

25 And there shall be signs in the sun, and in the moon, and in the
stars; and upon the earth distress of nations, with perplexity; the
sea and the waves roaring;

26 Men's hearts failing them for fear, and for looking after those
things which are coming on the earth: for the powers of heaven

shall be shaken.

27 And then shall they see the Son of man coming in a cloud with power and great glory.

28 And when these things begin to come to pass, then look up, and lift up your heads; for your redemption draweth nigh.

29 And he spake to them a parable; Behold the fig tree, and all the trees;

30 When they now shoot forth, ye see and know of your own selves that summer is now nigh at hand.

31 So likewise ye, when ye see these things come to pass, know ye that the kingdom of God is nigh at hand.

So, while nobody knows when Christ will come again, there are certain "heads ups" that Christ says can be a warning. However, as we already pointed out, Paul looked at the world he lived in and thought Christ's reappearing was close at hand. Yet, nearly two thousand years have passed by since Paul's day and He has not come. I know that it is hard to think things can get worse than they are today, yet it seems mankind is on a steady path downward. Things look better for a while then disintegrate. We take the proverbial one step forward then two steps back. There is not much we can do except minister to our fellow followers of Christ while keeping an eye on the Eastern horizon (we are taught elsewhere in the scriptures that He will come out of the East), looking for Christ to come and put an end to the folly most men and women call a way of living.

32 Verily I say unto you, This generation shall not pass away, till all be fulfilled.

33 Heaven and earth shall pass away: but my words shall not pass away.

34 And take heed to yourselves, lest at any time your hearts be

overcharged with surfeiting, and drunkenness, and cares of this life, and so that day come upon you unawares.

35 For as a snare shall it come on all them that dwell on the face of the whole earth.

36 Watch ye therefore, and pray always, that ye may be accounted worthy to escape all these things that shall come to pass, and to stand before the Son of man.

37 And in the day time he was teaching in the temple; and at night he went out, and abode in the mount that is called the mount of Olives.

38 And all the people came early in the morning to him in the temple, for to hear him.

What was Christ saying and teaching that all these people were drawn unto Him? Not the end of the world as was the topic of the few previous verses. That teaching was sad for it dealt with Christs death and not very uplifting for it also dealt with Jerusalem being destroyed. Also it was mainly for his disciples, anyway. Nor was he teaching the law and doctrines, if people wanted that they only had to speak to the Pharisee that lived next door or down the street. No, Christ must have been teaching the gospel of salvation, the gospel of loving thy neighbor. He must have been preaching the Sermon on the Mount again to this new audience.

Chapter 22

1 Now the feast of unleavened bread drew nigh, which is called the Passover.

2 And the chief priests and scribes sought how they might kill him; for they feared the people.

3 Then entered Satan into Judas surnamed Iscariot, being of the number of the twelve.

4 And he went his way, and communed with the chief priests and captains, how he might betray him unto them.

5 And they were glad, and covenanted to give him money.

6 And he promised, and sought opportunity to betray him unto them in the absence of the multitude.

Today, and almost every day, we see our political leaders trying to cover up their misdeeds. They hide them from the masses for fear of what might happen to them if the average citizen found out what they really are up to. Here, with the traitor Judas' help, Jewish leaders are attempting to capture and eventually kill Christ, but in some way such that it will not become public knowledge.

Those that want to blame the Jews for Christ's death should read these verses. It is true that the people plotting against Jesus were Jews. But they were not the average Jew. They were not the people. They were a few power-hungry leaders. If it was the Jewish people who wanted Christ dead there would be no need for scheming with Judas to do their dirt "in the absence of the multitude." They could just walk up to him anytime and take Him away to their torture chambers, and for

The average man is hungry for the light, the love, and the hope that Christ's church offers. It is those who see this as a threat to their positions and sinecures that seek to discredit Christ and His teaching, or to pervert those teachings so that gospel loses its force and power to save.

7 Then came the day of unleavened bread, when the passover must be killed.

8 And he sent Peter and John, saying, Go and prepare us the passover, that we may eat.

9 And they said unto him, Where wilt thou that we prepare?

10 And he said unto them, Behold, when ye are entered into the city, there shall a man meet you, bearing a pitcher of water; follow him into the house where he entereth in.

11 And ye shall say unto the goodman of the house, The Master saith unto thee, Where is the guestchamber, where I shall eat the passover with my disciples?

12 And he shall shew you a large upper room furnished: there make ready.

13 And they went, and found as he had said unto them: and they made ready the passover.

I find it interesting that here and when he came into Jerusalem riding on a burro, Christ prophesied in such detail. I am not sure of the reason. Maybe he knew that if given much latitude the disciples would bungle the job. It wasn't until He had gone back to heaven and the Holy Spirit fill these men that they were transformed and then went out an turned the Roman Empire on its head.

14 And when the hour was come, he sat down, and the twelve apostles

with him.

15 And he said unto them, With desire I have desired to eat this passover with you before I suffer:

16 For I say unto you, I will not any more eat thereof, until it be fulfilled in the kingdom of God.

17 And he took the cup, and gave thanks, and said, Take this, and divide it among yourselves:

18 For I say unto you, I will not drink of the fruit of the vine, until the kingdom of God shall come.

19 And he took bread, and gave thanks, and brake it, and gave unto them, saying, This is my body which is given for you: this do in remembrance of me.

20 Likewise also the cup after supper, saying, This cup is the new testament in my blood, which is shed for you.

21 But, behold, the hand of him that betrayeth me is with me on the table.

22 **And truly the Son of man goeth, as it was determined: but woe unto that man by whom he is betrayed!**

Judas was only doing what had been prophesied. Yet he is accountable for his deeds. God may know ahead of time what choices we will make, but that does not relieve us of our responsibility for those choices. Nor will we be able to say "the devil made me do it." We make choices and we will be called to answer for those choices. We can serve ourselves or our fellow creatures. Those that choose others over self have riches awaiting us in heaven.

23 And they began to inquire among themselves, which of them it was that should do this thing.

24 And there was also a strife among them, which of them should be accounted the greatest.

25 And he said unto them, The kings of the Gentiles exercise lordship over them; and they that exercise authority upon them are called

benefactors.

26 But ye shall not be so: but he that is greatest among you, let him be as the younger; and he that is chief, as he that doth serve.

27 **For whether is greater, he that sitteth at meat, or he that serveth? is not he that sitteth at meat? but I am among you as he that serveth.**

The church and the kingdom of God are just the opposite of the world. In the Old Testament Book of Micah we read in verse eight of the sixth chapter, "He hath shewed thee, O man, what is good; and what doth the LORD require of thee, but to do justly, and to love mercy, and to walk humbly with thy God," How unlike our current leaders, who love power, delight is stepping on the little man, and are proud and puffed up about themselves. Heavenly Father and Jesus are not interested in having followers who have inflated opinions of themselves, who are proud of their whatever it is that fills them with pride. We need to cast aside the things we feel make us better men and women than our brethren and sisters.

28 Ye are they which have continued with me in my temptations.

29 And I appoint unto you a kingdom, as my Father hath appointed unto me;

30 That ye may eat and drink at my table in my kingdom, and sit on thrones judging the twelve tribes of Israel.

31 **And the Lord said, Simon, Simon, behold, Satan hath desired to have you, that he may sift you as wheat:**

32 **But I have prayed for thee, that thy faith fail not: and when thou art converted, strengthen thy brethren.**

Satan may desire Heavenly Father to give him power over us, but I do not believe Heavenly Father does so. Not when we have the Holy Spirit abiding in us. A loving father does not give his children into the hands of a evil being like Satan. Whence come our trials then?

Mostly, I believe they come from our own folly. We bring on most of our problems all by ourselves, and don't need Lucifer to help. I also believe that, as the scriptures teach, Men love darkness better than light because their deeds are evil. We do not need much help to do wrong, it's doing right that runs counter to our instincts and requires help. It is easier for those who do not follow Christ's example of loving ministering to work us harm than to do well by us. As for sickness, it seems to be our lot in life to deal with physical maladies. I don't know the answer to that, just that I have more than my share.

It is interesting that Christ says He prayed for Peter. There is all sorts of inferences to draw from these words of the Master. First, not only did He pray for Peter but He expects that prayer to be answered. He says "when" Peter is converted he is to strengthen his brethren. Not "if" but "when." That "when" has further meaning, that being that Peter has yet to be converted. Three years he has walked and talked to Christ and yet he is not fully committed. He looks up to Christ. He had to, to stick around that long. He had to have seen the miracles too. So it seems to me Peter had an intellectual conversion already. However, he also had some preconceived ideas about what the Messiah was to do and he was trying in his head to fit Christ into that mold. He was trying to put the proverbial square peg in the round hole. He had to give up those ideas and accept the Christ that he knew and not the Christ that he desired.

33 And he said unto him, Lord, I am ready to go with thee, both into prison, and to death.

34 And he said, I tell thee, Peter, the cock shall not crow this day, before that thou shalt thrice deny that thou knowest me.

35 And he said unto them, When I sent you without purse, and scrip, and shoes, lacked ye any thing? And they said, Nothing.

36 Then said he unto them, But now, he that hath a purse, let him take it, and likewise his scrip: and he that hath no sword, let him sell his

garment, and buy one.

37 For I say unto you, that this that is written must yet be accomplished in me, And he was reckoned among the transgressors: for the things concerning me have an end.

38 And they said, Lord, behold, here are two swords. And he said unto them, It is enough.

39 And he came out, and went, as he was wont, to the mount of Olives; and his disciples also followed him.

40 And when he was at the place, he said unto them, Pray that ye enter not into temptation.

41 And he was withdrawn from them about a stone's cast, and kneeled down, and prayed,

42 **Saying, Father, if thou be willing, remove this cup from me: nevertheless not my will, but thine, be done.**

43 **And there appeared an angel unto him from heaven, strengthening him.**

44 **And being in an agony he prayed more earnestly: and his sweat was as it were great drops of blood falling down to the ground.**

Christ looked forward to his death at the hands of the Romans with real dread. It was not going to be a pleasant way to die and he knew it. He would sweat as it were great drops of blood as he prayed and counted down the minutes till Judas and the Priests would arrive with their servants to take Him prisoner.

Contemplating our death is not something many of us do with detachment. Our instinct is to keep living as long as possible. A few years ago, I had a bad fall and broke my hip and had to have surgery. As they were taking me into the operating room, I knew that going under the knife was risky at any age, but for a man in his late sixties much more so. I looked at those people gathered round me in green surgical outfits and stared up at the bright lights. I felt comforted as they took a warmed blanket and put it over me. The smell of disinfectant was on the air. I lay there and thought to myself that these might be the last things I ever saw, smelled, and felt. However, I did not fear what was going to happen or dying on that operating table. I prayed to Heavenly Father and told Him if he wanted me to die here it was okay and I was ready to go. I did not fear death. I was ready for it if it came. To this day I am proud of myself and how I confronted my own mortality and felt no dread as they put an IV in me and told me to count back from 100 and the world faded out.

However, years earlier I watched my father die by degrees as Alzheimer's Disease took his mind a little at a time until he no longer knew his family or much of anything. At the same time cancer ate away at his physical health. Dying like that scares me something awful. It is not death that frightens me, it is how I get there. It is how I die that has me very concerned. Confronted with such an ending as my father endured, I would cower in fear.

That must have been some of the reason Christ asked if the cup of death, at the hands of the Romans, could be taken away. I don't believe it was death that scared Him, it was how He was to die. I will deal more with his feelings about death when we get to his actual crucifixion.

45 And when he rose up from prayer, and was come to his disciples, he found them sleeping for sorrow,

46 And said unto them, Why sleep ye? rise and pray, lest ye enter into temptation.

47 And while he yet spake, behold a multitude, and he that was called Judas, one of the twelve, went before them, and drew near unto Jesus to kiss him.

48 But Jesus said unto him, Judas, betrayest thou the Son of man with a kiss?

49 When they which were about him saw what would follow, they said unto him, Lord, shall we smite with the sword?

50 And one of them smote the servant of the high priest, and cut off his right ear.

51 And Jesus answered and said, Suffer ye thus far. And he touched his ear, and healed him.

52 Then Jesus said unto the chief priests, and captains of the temple, and the elders, which were come to him, Be ye come out, as against a thief, with swords and staves?

53 **When I was daily with you in the temple, ye stretched forth no hands against me: but this is your hour, and the power of darkness.**

More proof that it was not the Jewish people that wanted Him dead, it was the rulers that saw Him as a threat that had to be removed.

54 **Then took they him, and led him, and brought him into the high priest's house. And Peter followed afar off.**

55 **And when they had kindled a fire in the midst of the hall, and were set down together, Peter sat down among them.**

56 **But a certain maid beheld him as he sat by the fire, and earnestly looked upon him, and said, This man was also with him.**

57 **And he denied him, saying, Woman, I know him not.**

58 **And after a little while another saw him, and said, Thou art also of them. And Peter said, Man, I am not.**

59 **And about the space of one hour after another confidently affirmed, saying, Of a truth this fellow also was with him: for he is a Galilaean.**

60 **And Peter said, Man, I know not what thou sayest. And immediately, while he yet spake, the cock crew.**

61 **And the Lord turned, and looked upon Peter. And Peter remembered the word of the Lord, how he had said unto him, Before the cock crow, thou shalt deny me thrice.**

62 **And Peter went out, and wept bitterly.**

I weep too, reading this. It is so poignant, so moving. Could this be the moment of Peter's conversion, that Christ foretold? It would not surprise me to find out that it was. It was surely an emotional moment. Yes, I think it was here or later when Christ appears to him after His death and resurrection while Peter is fishing.

63 And the men that held Jesus mocked him, and smote him.

64 And when they had blindfolded him, they struck him on the face, and asked him, saying, Prophesy, who is it that smote thee?

65 And many other things blasphemously spake they against him.

66 And as soon as it was day, the elders of the people and the chief priests and the scribes came together, and led him into their council, saying,

67 Art thou the Christ? tell us. And he said unto them, If I tell you, ye will not believe:

68 And if I also ask you, ye will not answer me, nor let me go.

69 Hereafter shall the Son of man sit on the right hand of the power of God.

70 Then said they all, Art thou then the Son of God? And he said unto them, Ye say that I am.

71 And they said, What need we any further witness? for we ourselves have heard of his own mouth.

Chapter 23

1 And the whole multitude of them arose, and led him unto Pilate.

2 And they began to accuse him, saying, We found this fellow perverting the nation, and forbidding to give tribute to Caesar, saying that he himself is Christ a King.

3 And Pilate asked him, saying, Art thou the King of the Jews? And he answered him and said, Thou sayest it.

4 Then said Pilate to the chief priests and to the people, I find no fault in this man.

5 And they were the more fierce, saying, He stirreth up the people, teaching throughout all Jewry, beginning from Galilee to this place.

6 When Pilate heard of Galilee, he asked whether the man were a Galilaean.

7 And as soon as he knew that he belonged unto Herod's jurisdiction, he sent him to Herod, who himself also was at Jerusalem at that time.

Pilate was a Roman ruling a people that did not want to be ruled by Rome. If he could foist Christ off on Herod so much the better. Pilate had not risen to the point he was at by molly coddling those ruled by Rome. He'd kill Jesus and loose no sleep over it if it came to that, which it would.

8 And when Herod saw Jesus, he was exceeding glad: for he was desirous to see him of a long season, because he had heard many things of him; and he hoped to have seen some miracle done by him.

9 Then he questioned with him in many words; but he answered him nothing.

10 And the chief priests and scribes stood and vehemently accused him.

11 And Herod with his men of war set him at nought, and mocked him, and arrayed him in a gorgeous robe, and sent him again to Pilate.

12 And the same day Pilate and Herod were made friends together: for before they were at enmity between themselves.

13 And Pilate, when he had called together the chief priests and the rulers and the people,

14 Said unto them, Ye have brought this man unto me, as one that perverteth the people: and, behold, I, having examined him before you, have found no fault in this man touching those things whereof ye accuse him:

15 No, nor yet Herod: for I sent you to him; and, lo, nothing worthy of death is done unto him.

16 I will therefore chastise him, and release him.

17 (For of necessity he must release one unto them at the feast.)

18 And they cried out all at once, saying, Away with this man, and release unto us Barabbas:

19 (Who for a certain sedition made in the city, and for murder, was cast into prison.)

20 **Pilate therefore, willing to release Jesus, spake again to them.**

21 **But they cried, saying, Crucify him, crucify him.**

22 **And he said unto them the third time, Why, what evil hath he done? I have found no cause of death in him: I will therefore chastise him, and let him go.**

23 **And they were instant with loud voices, requiring that he might be crucified. And the voices of them and of the chief priests prevailed.**

24 **And Pilate gave sentence that it should be as they required.**

How Pilate and those chief priests must dread the judgement day that is coming when we all will be asked to give an accounting of the lives we lived. At least each time we make a major decision we

should weigh the possible consequences, knowing that we will be held responsible for what we did.

25 And he released unto them him that for sedition and murder was cast into prison, whom they had desired; but he delivered Jesus to their will.

26 **And as they led him away, they laid hold upon one Simon, a Cyrenian, coming out of the country, and on him they laid the cross, that he might bear it after Jesus.**

I see two things here. Christ has been tortured to the point He is too weak to carry His own cross. The Son of God and he is treated that way. Horrible. Second, black people didn't receive much respect in those days either. As I read this they just grabbed him because he was black and made carry Christ's cross. I am thankful that we live in a day when that is changing to some extent. Things are not like they should be, but we are making slow progress. I see lots of Black men with a white woman. That would be very rare fifty years ago. I look for the day it is just as common to see a Black woman with a white man.

27 And there followed him a great company of people, and of women, which also bewailed and lamented him.

28 But Jesus turning unto them said, Daughters of Jerusalem, weep not for me, but weep for yourselves, and for your children.

29 For, behold, the days are coming, in the which they shall say, Blessed are the barren, and the wombs that never bare, and the paps which never gave suck.

30 Then shall they begin to say to the mountains, Fall on us; and to the hills, Cover us.

31 For if they do these things in a green tree, what shall be done in the dry?

32 And there were also two other, malefactors, led with him to be put to death.

33 And when they were come to the place, which is called Calvary, there they crucified him, and the malefactors, one on the right hand, and the other on the left.

34 Then said Jesus, Father, forgive them; for they know not what they do. And they parted his raiment, and cast lots.

35 And the people stood beholding. And the rulers also with them derided him, saying, He saved others; let him save himself, if he be Christ, the chosen of God.

36 And the soldiers also mocked him, coming to him, and offering him vinegar,

37 And saying, If thou be the king of the Jews, save thyself.

38 And a superscription also was written over him in letters of Greek, and Latin, and Hebrew, THIS IS THE KING OF THE JEWS.

39 **And one of the malefactors which were hanged railed on him, saying, If thou be Christ, save thyself and us.**

40 **But the other answering rebuked him, saying, Dost not thou fear God, seeing thou art in the same condemnation?**

41 **And we indeed justly; for we receive the due reward of our deeds: but this man hath done nothing amiss.**

42 **And he said unto Jesus, Lord, remember me when thou comest into thy kingdom.**

43 **And Jesus said unto him, Verily I say unto thee, To day shalt thou be with me in paradise.**

I have heard many say this is the way to be "saved." Others says something else. This man did not come down some aisle at an altar call after some spell binding sermon. He had no opportunity to be baptized. What he did was recognize his own unworthiness, that he was a sinner. He also recognized Christ as the Savior. He did that and Christ said they would be together in Paradise before the day was over. Rites like baptism can be done by proxy and taken care of later. The important thing was to recognize himself for what he was and Christ for who He was.

I have heard people deriding "deathbed conversions," saying they aren't real, that you have to live at least some of your life as a righteous person to prove your worthiness for salvation. Well, tell that to the thief on the cross. If there ever was a deathbed conversion, his was it, and if Christ is to be believed (and I think he is) that man went to paradise, even though his conversion took place just hours before he died.

**44 And it was about the sixth hour, and there was a darkness over all the earth until the ninth
hour.**

I have seen countless movies and religious films etc. that depict for us how Christ suffered both in the Garden of Gethsemane, at the hands of Pilate, the soldiers, and Herod, and then on Golgotha where he was crucified. But in the gospel accounts of the crucifixion we are given very little insight as to what was going on in His mind during the last few hours of his life. I can think of two insightful things He said that cast a light on what He was thinking as He hung between heaven and earth. He asked His Father to forgive those responsible for His crucifixion. That's not something you would expect accept from a divine personage like Christ. Second, He asked the Apostle John to take care of His mother, Mary. That is something a good human would do. In these two things we see He is both God and man.

However, I think we can find out of what he was thinking as He hung there buy looking in the Old Testament.

There we are told that God loved King David and that he was "A man after God's own heart." Heavenly Father made a covenant with David that the Messiah (Christ) would be a descendant of his. This was about the greatest honor Heavenly Father could bestow, and he gave it to David. David was a sinful man, and his moral compass leaves much to be desired. However, he was steadfast in his dedication to Heavenly Father. Never did he fall into the trap of imitating the kings and people of surrounding lands. He never worshiped a false god or had a statue of one set up, or in anyway honored idolatry. David was true to the commandment, "Thou shall have no other god before me." He is the King that the Jewish people still look up to today.

David was not just a warrior and king, he was a poet too. Most of the Psalms we find in the Old Testament are accredited to him. His psalms and others were collected in what we call The Book of Psalms which was sort of the Jewish people's hymnbook.

For his dedication and for the wonderful songs David composed in honor of Heavenly Father, and also because of his broken and contrite heart when he had sinned, and his earnest seeking after forgiveness, David was given a special insight into what the savior would suffer and endure to cover up those same sins David was so sorry to have committed. He was given a look into the mind of Christ as he hung on a cross paying for our sins.

Luke does not record it in his account of the crucifixion, but at one point, while Christ was on the cross He cried out "eli eli lama sabachthani" and when he did so, those gathered at the cross thought he was calling to Elijah to come and save Him from the cross. The cruel mockers that had come to see Him die laughed and said "Let's see if Elijah comes." In fact, Christ was not calling for Elijah. He was saying "My God, My God, why hast thou forsaken me."

We also find those words elsewhere in the scriptures. They appear in the 21st Psalm. In the first half of that Psalm David is given a privileged insight into the Saviors mind as he hung on the cross. I have cut and pasted the relevant sections of that Psalm below. Lets look into our Savior's mind and heart as he hung there on the cross.

Psalm 21

1 My God, my God, why hast thou forsaken me? why art thou so far from helping me, and from the words of my roaring?
2 O my God, I cry in the day time, but thou hearest not; and in the night season, and am not silent.

I think these words are the saddest and most poignant in the scriptures, they tell of suffering much more harsh than the pain of the beatings, the crown of thorns, or the nails driven through hands and feet. Christ is Heavenly Father's son. He often says they are one. But now the sins of mankind have been placed on His shoulders. Heavenly Father can no longer look on him as he bears those sins. This is the moment Christ most needs to feel the presence of His Heavenly Father and it is the moment He can't. In his despair He cries out "My God, My God why have you left me. Don't you hear me crying for you, don't you hear me roaring for you." I believe these are the loneliest words in the whole Bible, and we are the cause of them. Our sins and the rest of mankind's sins. They are placed on Christ and Heavenly Father turns away from Him. Is it any wonder that a few hours earlier Christ was saying "If it is possible, remove this cup from me. Don't make me go through this."

3 But thou art holy, O thou that inhabitest the praises of Israel.
4 Our fathers trusted in thee: they trusted, and thou didst deliver them.
5 They cried unto thee, and were delivered: they trusted in thee, and were not confounded.
6 **But I am a worm, and no man; a reproach of men, and despised of the people.**

7 <u>**All they that see me laugh me to scorn: they shoot out the lip, they shake the head, saying,**</u>
8 <u>**He trusted on the LORD that he would deliver him: let him deliver him, seeing he delighted in him.**</u>

It is not easy to be laughed at and pitied. It must be infinitely harder to have such scorn heaped on you as you are dying.

9 <u>**But thou art he that took me out of the womb: thou didst make me hope when I was upon my mother's breasts.**</u>
10 <u>**I was cast upon thee from the womb: thou art my God from my mother's belly.**</u>
11 <u>**Be not far from me; for trouble is near; for there is none to help.**</u>

Once more He vainly tries to convince Heavenly Father to return, to be there with him.

12 <u>**Many bulls have compassed me: strong bulls of Bashan have beset me round.**</u>
13 <u>**They gaped upon me with their mouths, as a ravening and a roaring lion.**</u>

This was written three thousand years ago, about something that was to happen two thousand years ago. Some of allusions are to things that we may not readily identify with. Yet I think we all can understand being surrounded by bulls. That can't be a comfortable situation. I remember when I was first married and crossing the country to visit family in California. My wife and I were in Texas, and not having the money for a motel, we went up a dirt road and into a stand of trees and camped out for the night on the ground in sleeping bags. We woke at first light to find ourselves surrounded by a herd of cattle. I am not sure if there were any bulls or not, but we were frightened they might for any reason charge us. Needless to say we tossed our sleeping bags into the car and got out of there asap. Christ was not just God, he was a man too. Being surrounded by wild animals that out weigh you by hundreds of pounds each has got to be a daunting experience.

Christ finds Himself on a cross and surrounded by enemies there to watch him die.

14 <u>**I am poured out like water, and all my bones are out of joint:**</u>

Imagine you have just been nailed to a cross. Nails driven through your hands, wrists, and ankles, and then that cross tipped up and dropped in a hole. The jarring of the cross hitting bottom of the hole pulls your arms out of joint adding a new level of pain.

<u>**my heart is like wax; it is melted in the midst of my bowels.**</u>

How His heart must have pounded in his chest.

15 **My strength is dried up like a potsherd; and my tongue cleaveth to my jaws; and thou hast brought me into the dust of death.**

A potsherd is a broken piece of pottery. In those days they did not, or rarely glazed pottery. Exposed to moisture the potsherd would drink it like a sponge. Christ is saying here he is thirsty. And what did they do for him, they gave him vinegar to drink, which would only make his thirst worse. Cruelty piled on cruelty.

16 For dogs have compassed me: the assembly of the wicked have enclosed me: <u>**they pierced my hands and my feet.**</u>

17 I may tell all my bones: they look and stare upon me.

People of Christ's time were mostly of a modest sort. They wore clothing that covered most of their bodies. Hands, face, and feet might be seen easy enough, and maybe arms too. However, for the most part they kept themselves covered. However, Christ was stripped of his clothing when he was crucified. Paintings always depict Him with just a loin cloth cover His privates. I am not sure He would have been afforded even that level of respect. Cloth was valuable. It all had to be made by hand, and even a loin cloth would be the product of hours' of labor. More likely He was naked on His cross. He could look down on Himself and see all His bones beneath stretched skin. One more humiliation to be heaped on His suffering person.

18 They part my garments among them, and cast lots upon my vesture.

We are told in another gospel that Christ had a special garment he wore that had been woven as a single piece and was seamless, thus making it of a higher value. Rather than cut it into pieces to give the executioners each a piece to sell, they gambled to see who would get the whole thing. Again, man's cruelty to man is evident. However, I wonder if Satan did not have a hand in some of this cruelty. He must have known that Christ was carrying out Heavenly Father's plan for mankind's salvation, and that this crucifixion was his defeat. It was the crushing of his skull that had been promised way back in Garden of Eden when he had tempted Adam and Eve to sin. He had to know the game was over, he was done, but being the cruel being he is, he must have strived to make the price paid to be as painful, both physically and spiritually as possible.

19 But be not thou far from me, O Lord: O my strength, haste

<u>**thee to help me.**</u>

20 <u>**Deliver my soul from the sword; my darling from the power of the dog.**</u>

21 <u>**Save me from the lion's mouth: for thou hast heard me from the horns of the unicorns.**</u>

These final words must come from the end of the crucifixion. The suffering is over, the price for sin paid, Christ is about to die, and these final three verses are the thoughts of the victor who has suffered and is now about to be freed. In but a moment he will commend His spirit to Heavenly Father and say "It is finished."

I want to close this section with a quote from Thomas Brooks (1608 to 1655), a Puritan preacher. It is from his book, <u>Precious Remedies Against Satan's Devices</u>. In it he writes of sin and its culmination on Calvary as follows: <u>That He that binds the devils in chains be tempted, that He, whose is the world and the fullness thereof, should hunger and thirst; that the God of strength be weary, the judge of all flesh, condemned, the God of all life put to death; that He that is one with the father should cry out of misery, "My God, My God," why hast thou forsaken me?" That He that had the keys of death and hell at His gridle should lie imprisoned in the sepulcher of another, having in His lifetime no where to lay His head, nor after death to lay His body; that that head, before which the angels cast down their crowns, should be crowned with thorns, and those eyes, purer than the sun, be put out by the darkness of death; those ears that hear nothing but the hallelujahs of saints and angels, hear the blasphemy of the multitude, that face, which was fairer than the sons of men to be spit upon, that mouth and tongue that spoke never as man spoke, accused for blasphemy; those hands that freely waved the scepter of heaven, nailed to the cross for man's sins, each sense annoyed, His feeling or touching with a spear and nails, His smell with stinking flavor, being crucified about Golgotha, the place of skulls, His taste with vinegar and gall, His</u>

45 And the sun was darkened, and the veil of the temple was rent in the midst.

46 And when Jesus had cried with a loud voice, he said, Father, into thy hands I commend my spirit: and having said thus, he gave up the ghost.

47 Now when the centurion saw what was done, he glorified God, saying, Certainly this was a righteous man.

48 And all the people that came together to that sight, beholding the things which were done, smote their breasts, and returned.

49 And all his acquaintance, and the women that followed him from Galilee, stood afar off, beholding these things.

50 **And, behold, there was a man named Joseph, a counseller; and he was a good man, and a just:**

51 **(The same had not consented to the counsel and deed of them;) he was of Arimathaea, a city of the Jews: who also himself waited for the kingdom of God.**

52 **This man went unto Pilate, and begged the body of Jesus.**

53 **And he took it down, and wrapped it in linen, and laid it in a sepulchre that was hewn in stone, wherein never man before was laid.**

He suffered greatly that day, but the suffering is over, the price for sin has been paid. No longer does He have to be treated with disrespect. He gets a new grave, not one full of dead men's bones. (In those days, when a Jew died he/she was laid out on a slab in a small cave. After a year or so family would come and collect the bones that were all that would be left by that time. These bones would go into a small stone box that sometimes had the name of the individual carved into the stone. The box of bones would then be stacked in one corner of the grave cave with the boxes of bones from previous deaths and the slab was then ready for the next person who died to be laid out.) Christ instead gets a new grave and not one He has to share with others who died at some earlier time.

54 And that day was the preparation, and the sabbath drew on.
55 And the women also, which came with him from Galilee, followed after, and beheld the sepulchre, and how his body was laid.
56 And they returned, and prepared spices and ointments; and rested the sabbath day according to the commandment.

Chapter 24

1   Now upon the first day of the week, very early in the morning, they came unto the sepulchre, bringing the spices which they had prepared, and certain others with them.

Way back at or shortly after His birth the Wise Men visited the baby Jesus. Two of the gifts they gave him were frankincense and myrrh. The main usages of these were for preparing the dead for burial. Both were aromatics that were use to cut back on the scent of death and decomposition. It is ironic that the wise men would give such gifts to a child. However, Jesus is the one person that was born, not to live, but to die. We all have purposes for being born and living. Christ's purpose was to die for our sins.

2   And they found the stone rolled away from the sepulchre.
3   And they entered in, and found not the body of the Lord Jesus.
4   And it came to pass, as they were much perplexed thereabout, behold, two men stood by them in shining garments:
5   And as they were afraid, and bowed down their faces to the earth, they said unto them, Why seek ye the living among the dead?
6   He is not here, but is risen: remember how he spake unto you when he was yet in Galilee,
7   Saying, The Son of man must be delivered into the hands of sinful men, and be crucified, and the third day rise again.
8   And they remembered his words,

How do they forget these things?

9   And returned from the sepulchre, and told all these things unto the

eleven, and to all the rest.

10 It was Mary Magdalene, and Joanna, and Mary the mother of James, and other women that were with them, which told these things unto the apostles.

Notice it was Mary Magdalene that is mentioned first. I do not believe that is happenstance. She takes preeminence because, as I have mentioned earlier in this commentary, I believe Mary was Christ's wife. Another gospel reveals that she is the first person he appears to after his resurrection. Again, why? The answer, she was his wife.

11 And their words seemed to them as idle tales, and they believed them not.

12 Then arose Peter, and ran unto the sepulchre; and stooping down, he beheld the linen clothes laid by themselves, and departed, wondering in himself at that which was come to pass.

The Shroud of Turin? Very possibly.

13 And, behold, two of them went that same day to a village called Emmaus, which was from Jerusalem about **threescore furlongs**.

A furlong is an eighth of a mile and a score is twenty, so "threescore furlongs" would be about seven and a half miles.

14 And they talked together of all these things which had happened.
15 And it came to pass, that, while they communed together and reasoned, Jesus himself drew near, and went with them.
16 But their eyes were holden that they should not know him.
17 And he said unto them, What manner of communications are these that ye have one to another, as ye walk, and are sad?
18 And the one of them, whose name was Cleopas, answering said unto him, Art thou only a stranger in Jerusalem, and hast not known

the things which are come to pass therein these days?

19 And he said unto them, What things? And they said unto him, Concerning Jesus of Nazareth, which was a prophet mighty in deed and word before God and all the people:

20 And how the chief priests and our rulers delivered him to be condemned to death, and have crucified him.

21 But we trusted that it had been he which should have redeemed Israel: and beside all this, to day is the third day since these things were done.

22 Yea, and certain women also of our company made us astonished, which were early at the sepulchre;

23 And when they found not his body, they came, saying, that they had also seen a vision of angels, which said that he was alive.

24 And certain of them which were with us went to the sepulchre, and found it even so as the women had said: but him they saw not.

25 Then he said unto them, **O fools, and slow of heart to believe all that the prophets have spoken:**

Those words have meaning for us today, also. Are we slow to believe and follow the words spoken by our modern day prophet? God has not left us without council, but it does us no good if we do not heed what he tells us.

26 Ought not Christ to have suffered these things, and to enter into his glory?

27 And beginning at Moses and all the prophets, he expounded unto them in all the scriptures the things concerning himself.

28 And they drew nigh unto the village, whither they went: and he made as though he would have gone further.

29 But they constrained him, saying, Abide with us: for it is toward evening, and the day is far spent. And he went in to tarry with them.

30 **And it came to pass, as he sat at meat with them, he took bread, and blessed it, and brake, and gave to them.**

31 And their eyes were opened, and they knew him; and he vanished out of their sight.

32 And they said one to another, Did not our heart burn within us, while he talked with us by the way, and while he opened to us the scriptures?

33 And they rose up the same hour, and returned to Jerusalem, and found the eleven gathered together, and them that were with them,

34 Saying, The Lord is risen indeed, and hath appeared to Simon.

35 And they told what things were done in the way, and how he was known of them in breaking of bread.

I am assuming that He broke and passed the bread in the same manner He had done so three day earlier at the Last Supper, and that is when they realized they were sitting with Christ and he was indeed alive just as Mary had told them.

This brings up a question: were the twelve the only followers of Christ at the last supper? The one man of these two who is definitely identified is Cleopas. He was not one of the twelve. His name does not appear on Luke's list of the apostles. The other's name was probably Simon. He too was not an apostle, for we are told that when the two men returned to Jerusalem they went to see the eleven apostles that were left.

Yet in Emmaus, when Christ broke and passed the bread the two men eating with Him suddenly knew who He was. How so, if they had not been at the Last Supper? Now, we know the room they used for the Last Supper was large. We are told so, and in fact, in the Book of Acts we are told that on the day of Pentecost that there were a hundred and twenty people gathered in that same room. Why the big room? Could it not be to make room for other tables? One for the women followers of

Christ. Why should they be left out? They shouldn't. And why not more tables for other men followers of Jesus. So, it seems to me the evidence points to there being a head table where Christ and the twelve ate, and other tables where other followers and disciples ate. I am not sure this is an important observation on my part, but it is interesting one, and nothing I can remember reading previously having read brings up the possibility.

I like the idea too. A last supper for the twelve, but not them alone. A last supper for Him and those most loyally following Him. I like a Last Supper where they are all included, and none excluded.

36 **And as they thus spake, Jesus himself stood in the midst of them, and saith unto them, Peace be unto you.**
37 **But they were terrified and affrighted, and supposed that they had seen a spirit.**
38 **And he said unto them, Why are ye troubled? and why do thoughts arise in your hearts?**
39 **Behold my hands and my feet, that it is I myself: handle me, and see; for a spirit hath not flesh and bones, as ye see me have.**
40 **And when he had thus spoken, he shewed them his hands and his feet.**
41 **And while they yet believed not for joy, and wondered, he said unto them, Have ye here any meat?**
42 **And they gave him a piece of a broiled fish, and of an honeycomb.**
43 **And he took it, and did eat before them.**

Asking them to handle Him and His eating the fish and honeycomb were done to show that He was a flesh and blood creature. I believe He is still a flesh and blood creature, with a body like yours and mine. Heavenly Father too. Only the Holy Spirit has no body.

44 And he said unto them, These are the words which I spake unto you, while I was yet with you, that all things must be fulfilled, which were written in the law of Moses, and in the prophets, and in the psalms, concerning me.

45 Then opened he their understanding, that they might understand the scriptures,

46 And said unto them, Thus it is written, and thus it behoved Christ to suffer, and to rise from the dead the third day:

47 And that repentance and remission of sins should be preached in his name among all nations, beginning at Jerusalem.

48 And ye are witnesses of these things.

49 And, behold, I send the promise of my Father upon you: **but tarry ye in the city of Jerusalem, until ye be endued with power from on high.**

50 **And he led them out as far as to Bethany, and he lifted up his hands, and blessed them.**

51 **And it came to pass, while he blessed them, he was parted from them, and carried up into heaven.**

52 **And they worshipped him, and returned to Jerusalem with great joy:**

53 **And were continually in the temple, praising and blessing God. Amen.**

They had to wait almost forty days, till the Feast of Pentecost, at which time they were filled with the Holy Spirit and began preaching the gospel and started a church that would turn the Roman world upside down.

I thought a fitting ending for this book might be a few short but earnest quotes from David, whom God loved and said he was a man after his own heart. As we mentioned before, David was a sinful man. Heavenly Father told him he could not build His temple for that

Psalm 25:4 Shew me thy ways, O LORD; teach me thy paths.

Psalm 119: 34 Give me understanding, and I shall keep thy law; yea, I shall observe it with my whole heart.

Psalm 119:125 I am thy servant; Oh grant me understanding.

It is my hope that you will make those words of David your prayer, and the things I have learned by writing this commentary, and hopefully, you have gleaned from reading them will make us all better and more worthy followers of Christ.

When Moses went up on Sinai to receive the Ten Commandments we are told that the finger of God wrote them on the stone tablets. In such a case we can be pretty sure that they would be error free. But what of the words in this Gospel or the others?

If the only version of the scriptures we had was the King James Version, or some other modern version we would not have a difficulty. It all sounds alike, but when we go back and look at the scriptures in their original form and language it is obvious, we are dealing with more than one author. The Gospel of John reads like a elementary school book while verbiage in The Epistle to the Hebrews is more like that of a college text. We are taught (and I think, rightfully so) that our Heavenly Father is unchanging. Yet if we look at His supposed writings that is not the case. To deal with this difficulty, most of those who believe the Bible to be inspired word for word, hold that the actual language of the scriptures is inspired by God through the Holy Spirit in the form of what might be called divine dictation, and in order to explain these differences they have decided that while God was using an individual to write the scriptures He would adopt that person's vocabulary and verbal mannerisms so that what was written would read like it had come from the person whose hand held the pen when in actuality it came from God.

As an example, I like the word "however" and use it too often in my writing. Just a personal foible. Now, according to the version of inspiration explained above, if Heavenly Father were to use me to write some scripture, He would adopt my weakness for howevers and the work produced would have a generous sprinkling of the word even though He knows the word appears excessively and thus makes the writing technically poor.

This is what is taught in theological schools and Bible colleges.

Sort of convoluted, right? Yet how else do they account for the stylistic differences to be found in the different books of the Scriptures? If you want to believe every word came from God and at the same time believe that God is unchanging you have to come up with some such explanation, as that delineated above.

I, for one, find it too much of a stretch. I think there must be some other explanation. I think the idea that Heavenly Father dictates the scriptures word for word is just an idea holding over from the Protestant Reformation and John Calvin and others like him. They believed that we were all puppets on strings, that our actions were predetermined. They had the idea that we were all just following a planned path. They thought God took absolute control of the words that appear in the scriptures. They also believed that when the Apostle John put the last period after the last word of the Book of Revelation, that God shut up. He no longer spoke to His people. He had given them the Bible and it had all they needed to know. They felt it was more important to hold to some creed or catechism than to have a personal relationship with Christ. They fought wars based on different ideas based on Scriptures. Such convictions, however, dictated the need for completely error free Scriptures. I mean if you are going to use a document to dictate how you live your life or why you kill your neighbor, it had better be correct. Right?

But, then here comes Luke saying that there are many versions of Christ's life being circulated in the Church. He implies someone needs to set the record straight, and he can do so because he claims a "perfect understanding" from the beginning. His words do not seem to lend themselves to the idea that he's going to sit down, take up a pen and the words will come to him by inspiration so he can then put them down. In the first sentence of his gospel he claims this perfect understanding and to have had it a long time. He does not need to take dictation from God, he is like most authors in that he knows where he is going with his book, and what he is going to write before he puts the first word to paper. If this is the case then inspiration must be somewhat different than we have been taught.

Luke joined the church sometime after its formation. It is most likely he never crossed paths with Christ. Yet here he comes along and claims to have this perfect understanding and to have had it for quite some time. How could he have acquired it? Could the Holy Spirit have somehow taught him the details of Christ's life on earth, then turned him loose to write the story he had been taught? Is it possible that this is the form that inspiration took for the writing of his gospel? I do not know, but it seems to be more plausible that the first explanation

This is not to imply that the scriptures are not the word of God. I believe they are. However, I am simply pointing out that the manner in which the inspiration came to Luke seems to be at variance with the orthodox view.

Another point to make here is that inspiration can come in different ways and places. As we will see in this first chapter of Luke, it can come from an angel, it can be poetic, it can seem spontaneous or thought out. The important thing is not the how, it is that God does speak to His people. He can tell us things out loud, or in a still small voice. He can put thoughts in our head, a burning in our chest, speak to us through the scriptures, prophets, or experiences. We are never alone. God is there, beside us, ready to guide us, or better still, He is there wanting to guide us, desiring to guide us. And He will too, if we just let Him.